11

LEICESTER TRAMWAYS

Colin Barker

Series editor Robert J. Harley

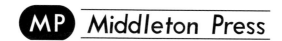

MP Middleton Press

Front cover: Delegates who had been attending a five-day Jehovah's Witnesses conference in September 1941 queue into the roadway to board cars travelling towards the city centre; note some are carrying gas masks. The location is Hill Top, London Road, close to the junction with Evington Road, with Cars 39 and 150 in view; a third tram can be seen in the distance. Car 39, destined for Narborough Road is in a simplified livery introduced in 1937, whilst Car 150, en route to Fosse Road via Great Central Street, is in the old livery. Note the wartime features of masked headlight, the word 'Leicester' painted out, and white bumper to help others in the wartime blackout. All the buildings on the right still exist. (Leicester Evening Mail/Leicester Transport Heritage Trust)

Back cover: A lunchtime view of Car 138 passing the departure arches of the Midland Station in London Road whilst on a special duty. The current station building was built by the Midland Railway between 1892 and 1894, replacing earlier facilities which had been gradually extended over the years. The header at the top of the notice board on the right has had the letters LMS (London Midland and Scottish Railway) painted over resulting from the formation of British Railways on 1st January 1948, which was part of the post war Labour Government's nationalisation programme. (F.N.T. Lloyd-Jones/Online Transport Archive)

The cover colours of maroon and cream represents the livery Leicester used.

Published September 2023

ISBN 978 1 910356 83 8

© Middleton Press Ltd, 2023

Cover design and Photographic enhancement Deborah Esher
Production Cassandra Morgan

Published by
    Middleton Press Ltd
    Camelsdale Road
    Haslemere
    Surrey
    GU27 3RJ
Tel: 01730 813169
Email: info@middletonpress.co.uk
www.middletonpress.co.uk

Printed and bound by CPI Group (UK) Ltd, Croydon, CR0 4YY

CONTENTS

ABBREVIATIONS:

AEC	Associated Equipment Company
EE	English Electric
ER&TCW	Electric Railway & Tramway Carriage Works Limited
LCT	Leicester City Transport
MCCW	Metropolitan-Cammell Carriage and Wagon Company Limited
PAYE	Pay As You Enter
UEC	United Electric Car Company

UEC was successor to ER&TCW, and was a subsidiary part of Dick, Kerr; eventually absorbed into EE.

INTRODUCTION AND ACKNOWLEDGMENTS

This album is not intended to be a detailed history of the Leicester tramway systems, but more a nostalgic journey along the roads they served, and illustrating the vehicles that were operated. It also provides a feel for the street scenes in the period 1874 to 1949, illustrating how many have changed over the years.

Many of the pictures selected are derived from my postcard collection, the photographs taken by the late F.N.T. Lloyd-Jones provided by the Online Transport Archive, the collections of the National Tramway Museum, and the collection of Peter Newland via the Leicester Transport Heritage Trust. Others are from collections and individual photographers; where sources are known due accreditation has been given but, in some cases, it has been impossible to identify the photographer and/or copyright holder. I hope that it will be accepted that these images have been included to display the photographer's work to a wider audience.

Thanks go to David Bowler, and four members of the Leicester Transport Heritage Trust namely Peter Newland, Mike Greenwood, Chris Jinks and Steve Foxon for reading through the first draft, with their corrections and constructive suggestions, plus the Light Rail and Transit Association for allowing the use of the maps. The Motor Museum at Beaulieu helped with a number of car identifications. The electric tram map is derived from J.C. Gillham's Map 85 based on an original by K.W. Smith, dated August 1950, revised by M.S.W. Pearson in June 1970, and drawn by Roger Smith; Roger also researched and drew the horse tram map. My wife Maureen has given her usual support in preparing this album, particularly using her computer skills to provide a usable format for the publisher to work from.

HISTORICAL AND GEOGRAPHICAL BACKGROUND

Leicester is one of three large East Midlands cities, the others being Nottingham and Derby, with the River Soar running to the west of the city. It is the county town of Leicestershire, with the current population of circa 562,000, and with the National Forest also to the west. It is an important rail cross road with the main line from London St Pancras leading northwards to Derby, Nottingham and Sheffield, plus a line connecting Birmingham with the east, particularly to Peterborough and Stanstead Airport. The M1 Motorway, and the M69 to Coventry, are close to the western boundary.

It is believed there was an early Celtic settlement, and after the Romans had captured Leicestershire by 47AD the settlement thrived. During their occupation, the Fosse Way between Exeter and Lincoln was constructed, with stretches still followed today. After their departure in 407, the settlement suffered decline, but by 800 the town was revived by the Anglo Saxons. The Danes invaded in 877 and captured Leicester, but it had been recaptured by 918.

After the Norman occupation, the Domesday Book (1086) indicated a population of 1,500. The town was controlled by an earl who, via his agent, heavily taxed the inhabitants, and, by the early 1200s, Simon de Montfort was in control, introducing a vicious campaign against the Jewish population. Trade in the Middle Ages was mainly wool and leather processing with a weekly market, and an annual fair. By the mid 1400s the town had a corporation and mayor.

In the 1500-1600s, there were many outbreaks of the plague followed by the 1642-1651 Civil Wars between King Charles I and Parliament, with the former laying siege to the town. The numbers in the King's army greatly exceeded the town's Parliamentary inhabitants who were overwhelmed. The King's victory was soon reversed when the Royalists were defeated at the Battle of Naseby in 1645, with the town soon recovering. The population was circa 5,000 by 1670, and had more than trebled to 17,000 by 1800.

In the 1700s, pumps were installed at public water wells, and the Infirmary opened in 1771; on the industrial front the Soar Canal was completed in 1794 allowing the transport of coal and iron into the town, materials needed to support the fledgling engineering industry.

In the first half of the 1800s, there was substantial growth with the population rising to 68,000 by 1861, and amenities improved with the introduction of gas street lighting, paved streets and the creation of a police force. After experiencing a cholera epidemic in 1849, a Health Board was formed to oversee the installation of drains and sewers, the provision of a sewerage works, and a start in providing a piped water supply. In the second half of the 1800s, several public parks were opened, together with a public library and the creation of a town hall, plus a telephone exchange; a small number of streets were now lit by electricity.

In 1832, the Swannington to Leicester Railway was created to bring coal into the town, and in 1840 a line to Rugby was opened. These were followed by a line from Burton-on-Tent in 1849, and the opening of the southern section of the Midland Railway main line from London St Pancras in 1868. The Great Northern Railway built a line eastward towards Peterborough and Grantham from a terminal station in Belgrave Road in 1883, and the Great Central Railway opened a new northern line from London in 1899, with both companies building substantial stations in the town.

The 20th century saw continued rapid growth of the town, particularly engineering, with city status being granted in 1919, and the creation of a cathedral in 1927. The Palace Theatre was opened in 1901, the General Hospital in 1905, followed by the first cinema in 1910. From 1904, horse trams were replaced by electric vehicles, the last day of the former being 31st October 1904; the first motorbus was introduced in 1924.

In 1911, the Imperial Typewriter Company set up business in Leicester, enhancing the engineering profile of the town. The growth in engineering can be illustrated by the fact there were 6,000 employed in 1900, which had grown to 13,500 by 1939, and 29,000 in the 1950s. Whilst hosiery manufacturing remained important, newer industries including metal fabrication, electrical engineering, printing and food processing added to the profile.

The Council began building housing stock from early in the 1900s, which continued up to the Second World War, and in the peacetime that followed. The city only had limited bomb damage during the Second World War, unlike its near neighbour, Coventry. The last tram ran in 1949.

The University College Leicester gained university status in 1957, with the Leicester Polytechnic being formed from the old College of Art and Technology; the latter became the De Montfort University in 1992. On the retail front, three shopping centres were created, namely Haymarket in 1973, out of town Beaumont Leys in 1984 and The Shires, now known as Highcross, in 1991.

TITLES

Leicester's Horse Tramways

The Leicester Tramway Company Limited	1874 – 1877
The Leicester Tramway Company	1878 – 1901
Leicester Corporation Tramways	1901 – 1904

Leicester's Electric Tramways

Leicester Corporation Tramways	1904 – 1919
Leicester City Tramways	1919 – 1924
Leicester City Tramways and Motor Omnibus Department	1924 – 1935
City of Leicester Passenger Transport Department	1935 – 1937
Leicester City Transport	1937 – 1949

LIVERY

1904 – 1937:   Crimson lake and cream panels with gold leaf embellishments.

1937 onwards: Gradual change to maroon panels minus embellishments, and with unlined cream upper and lower window frames, plus the base of the lower deck panels and platforms.

   Later a narrow band of orange below the windows was added.

Post war: Cream at the base of lower deck panels and platforms discontinued.

PRE 1870

Prior to 1870, horse bus services operated in several towns and cities throughout the country, plus a small number of horse tram systems. The 1870 Tramway Act brought some structure on future development in allowing local authorities to grant licences to commercial companies to operate trams for a period of 21 years; the licence could be terminated at the end of this period, or every seven years thereafter. The threat of losing the licence often resulted in a lack of investment by some operators, particularly towards the end of the licence period.

SYSTEM HISTORY

A horse bus service was started by Messrs Brown and Bent in June 1863 travelling from the town centre along London Road to Oadby.

Promotors to build a tramway system reached agreement with the Corporation, and the Leicester Tramway Order of 1873 resulted in the Leicester Tramway Company being formed to operate horse drawn trams under the provisions of the 1870 Tramway Act. The first service opened on 24th December 1874 operating from the Clock Tower along Belgrave Road as far as the Folly Inn, and subsequently extended to Thurcaston Road at an unknown date. The following year, two new services were introduced, namely along Humberstone Road to Forest Road on 23th March, and along London Road to Victoria Park Road on 14th August.

In 1876, a trial was carried out using a steam tram engine to replace the horses drawing a passenger car; it was initially used along Belgrave Road, and subsequently to Stoneygate. The poor mechanical and speed performances resulted in the experiment being abandoned.

1878 saw the introduction of two new services, one out towards Aylestone as far as Grace Road on 7th June, and the second from Churchgate to Woodgate on 29th August; the latter used small 10-seater cars, and the service was called 'The Churchgate Express'. This year also saw the London Road service extended to Knighton Drive.

The original 11 cars were single deck purchased in 1874-75, plus six secondhand single deck vehicles from an unknown London operator; six were converted to double deck format.

A horse bus service from the tram terminus at Knighton Road to the New Inn in Oadby village had commenced by July 1878.

In 1884, powers were obtained to extend the Stoneygate tram service to Oadby, terminating near the parish church. The line was never built, and instead the company continued to operate the horse bus service to the village, although the terminus was changed to the Black Dog Hotel at an unknown date. The service was suspended from October 1885 to April 1887.

By 1886, the company had a maximum of 46 trams, and a further extension had been introduced along Humberstone Road to the Great Northern Railway station in Uppingham Road on 2nd August of that year; initially journeys were restricted to mainly morning duties.

In 1885 Mr Solomon Andrews expanded his horse bus interests from Cardiff to Leicester. On 14th September his first two services to Belgrave and Humberstone Road opened, and to

Highfields on 29th August 1887. These were in direct competition with the tramway company, who purchased Andrew's operations on 17th November 1887 for £8000. The purchase included 13 horse buses, 78 horses, a Belgrave depot and stables, plus some freehold land; the depot was later adapted for horse trams. Andrew's last duty was on the Highfields service, with the ownership changing with a mid-morning change of horses on 18th November 1887.

Under the provisions of the 1870 Act, after 28 years, the company was purchased by Leicester Corporation for £134,110 on 22nd August 1901, which included 39 trams, 30 horse buses, 375 horses, some real estate and 9 miles of track; full transfer was completed on 31st December 1901. Short term, the Corporation continued to operate the horse drawn services, with four cars being purchased from Nottingham Corporation in 1902 to supplement services.

In 1903, a sub committee was formed to consider what form of current collection should be used for the replacing electric trams, and recommended an overhead wire installation rather than a conduit system beneath the road surface. There was some opposition to the former, but the lower cost of £650,000 compared with over £1,000,000 for the conduit system resulted in the overhead system being adopted.

Plans were put in hand to design and install the track, particularly the layout around the Clock Tower, which was considered to be the most complex in the country. Two sample cars were ordered, one from the Electric Railway & Tramway Carriage Works Limited, and a second from local manufacturer Brush; the former found favour, and an order placed for 58 four-wheel open top double deck cars, followed by a further 40 similar cars, plus a water car.

The system opened on 18th May 1904 with due ceremony, and the public service commenced at 7.00pm. Over the next five and a half months, horse and electric cars operated side by side, with the first electrical services operating to Belgrave, Stoneygate, Clarendon Park (via Queens Road) and Melbourne Road. Services to Narborough Road, Western Park and the Fosse Road circulars were introduced on 12th July 1904, and that to Aylestone followed on 5th September; the Abbey Park Road Depot and workshops were also completed.

On 1st November 1904, the East Park Road and Humberstone services opened, which replaced the last horse trams. Next were the services to Groby Road on 22nd December 1904, and Melton Road on 18th June 1905, which resulted in an order for 21 cars with covered tops from UEC, who were the successor to Dick, Kerr; these were delivered in 1905.

The success of the electric trams resulted in increased traffic, so an order was placed with UEC for 20 open top cars and a water car, also delivered in 1905, plus an additional water car in 1909. The return to an open top design was because of poor ventilation on the previous covered delivery. In 1910, UEC designed a domed top cover, which overcame the ventilation problem, and 19 cars were so fitted.

1913-14 saw 20 balcony cars delivered comprising 10 from UEC and 10 from Brush. The former were built with larger platform areas for the introduction of a PAYE payment system of loading in March 1913 on the Narborough Road service. This method of payment was abandoned after 15 months. A decision was also taken to fit all open top cars with covers. By December 1915, 67 wartime female conductresses had been trained, with the last leaving in October 1919.

The 1914-18 War left the system in a poor state, with a backlog of track and vehicle maintenance, which was only rectified between 1920 and 1925. Work on the Welford Road service had begun before the war but was delayed because of it, and eventually opened on 26th September 1922.

Major post war plans for the expansion of the tram network did not come to fruition, with some services being covered by the Department's first motorbuses introduced from 24th July 1924. Experiments were carried out to give motormen and balcony passengers more weather protection, and Car 35, amongst others, was fitted with partial glazing around the balcony seats.

1920 saw the introduction of six cars built in the Department's workshops, and 12 supplied by EE. In 1923, an existing car was rebuilt to a fully enclosed design, and fitted with more powerful traction motors; subsequently all cars were then fitted with motorman vestibules and fully enclosed balconies, but to a simpler design.

At the west end of Humberstone Gate, there was a narrow opening next to the Bell Hotel, beyond which was a permanent way store, a traffic office and motor garage. In 1922, the small district depots at Stoneygate and Narborough Road were closed, and the Humberstone Gate establishment modified to accommodate 13 cars.

On 26th September 1922, a service opened to Clarendon Park via Welford Road followed on 22nd June 1924 by an extension along Abbey Park Road, and beyond the depot entrance, to reserved track in Blackbird Road. The extension catered for visitors to the Royal Show held on land above Anstey Lane. The final extension came on 31st March 1927 along Coleman Road from Uppingham Road, which comprised a mixture of single line with passing loops, and some reserved track.

In 1929-30, Belgrave Gate was widened from the centre to the London North Eastern Railway (ex-Great Northern Railway) station, and new double track introduced to replace the mixture of double and inter-laced metals. By this time, the Department was operating to a high standard with reconditioned vehicles, track and overhead.

Experiments were carried out with bow and pantograph current collectors on the Abbey Park and Groby Road services, but these designs were never implemented. Between 1931 and 1937, 23 cars were equipped with new underframes, which were extended to provide a wider platform area in an endeavour to speed up loading/unloading.

On 14th October 1933, service numbers 1 to 9 and 12 were fully implemented after earlier use on some services. The Melbourne Road service was abandoned on 13th December 1933 due to poor track condition, which comprised single line and passing loops. The national debate at the time as to whether trams should be replaced perhaps influenced this decision. Some authorities were replacing trams with trolleybuses, as in the case of Leicester's near neighbours, Derby and Nottingham. In Leicester, there was a similar debate, with the Electricity Department in favour of maintaining the municipal power station loading, whilst others were against, being particularly concerned about the heavy concentration of overhead infrastructure around the Clock Tower. The manager, Mr Ben England, recommended that the trams be replaced with 3-axle diesel motor-buses capable of carrying a similar number of passengers. This was implemented following a 21 to 14 vote.

In October 1938, a start was made on implementing the abandonment programme with the Coleman Road service being the first to go on 23rd October 1938, followed by King Richards Road on 2nd April 1939. The outbreak of the Second World War intervened, and there were no further conversions until 1945. The five war years were a difficult period for the Department in maintaining both vehicles and track, against the background of material shortages, lack of spare parts, and employees joining the armed forces.

1945 saw the recommencement of the abandonment programme, with the Clarendon Park via Welford Road closed on 2nd May. New motorbuses were in short supply after the war, so the Aylestone service was not converted until 5th January 1947. The Fosse Road service succumbed on 6th July the same year, to be followed by Western Park and Narborough Road on 21st November 1948.

In 1949, the Groby Road service closed on 23rd January, Blackbird Road on 13th March, and East Park Road circulars on 15th May, followed by Melton Road on 3rd July, and Belgrave/Stoneygate on 9th October. 9th November 1949 saw an appropriately decorated Car 58 close the system with a journey from Humberstone to the city centre, and then onwards to the Abbey Park Road depot with the official party. So ended 75 years of railed public transport in the city, with the electric trams having contributed over 45 years of service. Restored Car 76 can be seen at the Tramway Village, Crich, Derbyshire. In 1950, 20 trucks and underframes were sold to the Calcutta Tramway Company Limited.

➜   I. Horse Tramways map.

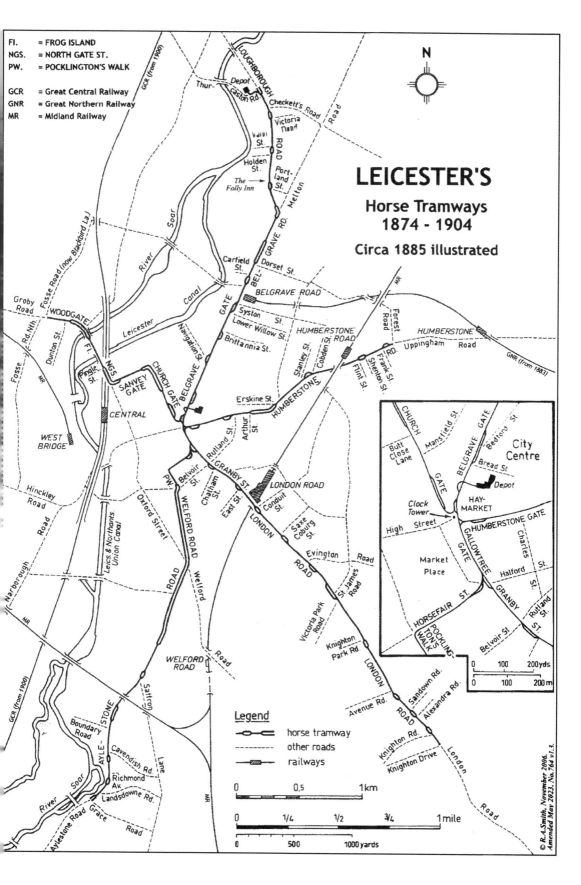

FI. = FROG ISLAND
NGS. = NORTH GATE ST.
PW. = POCKLINGTON'S WALK

GCR = Great Central Railway
GNR = Great Northern Railway
MR = Midland Railway

LEICESTER'S

Horse Tramways
1874 - 1904

Circa 1885 illustrated

Legend

⊶⊶ horse tramway
- - - other roads
▨▨▨ railways

0   0,5   1km

0   1/4   1/2   3/4   1mile

0   500   1000 yards

City Centre

© R.A.Smith, November 2006.
Amended May 2023. No. 764 v1.3.

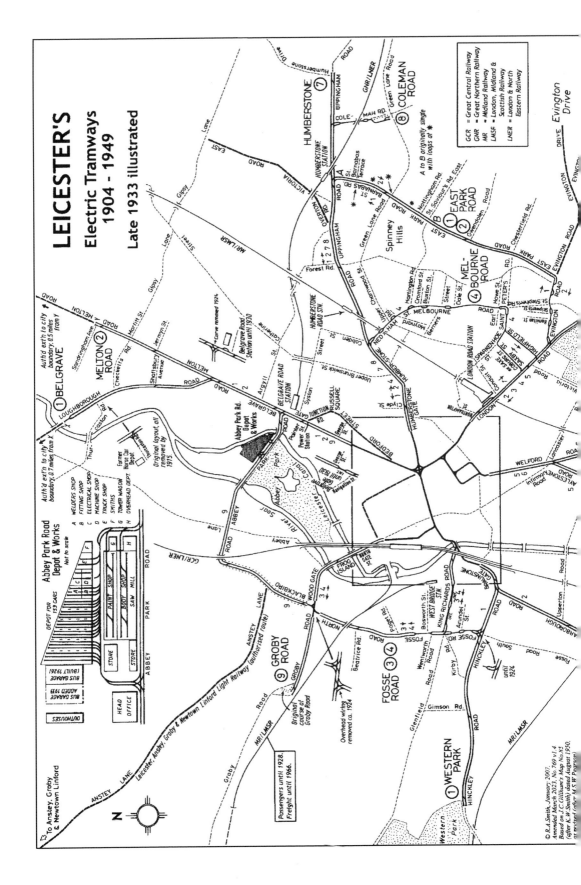

LEICESTER'S
Electric Tramways 1904 - 1949
Late 1933 illustrated

GCR = Great Central Railway
GNR = Great Northern Railway
MR = Midland Railway
LMSR = London, Midland & Scottish Railway
LNER = London & North Eastern Railway

A to B originally single with loops at *

Abbey Park Road Depot & Works
Not to scale

DEPOT FOR 159 CARS

A WELDERS SHOP
B FITTING SHOP
C ELECTRICAL SHOP
D MACHINE SHOP
E TRUCK SHOP
F SMITHS
G TOWER WAGON
H OVERHEAD DEPT.

PAINT SHOP
BODY SHOP
SAW MILL
STORE
HEAD OFFICE
OUTHOUSES

BUS GARAGE (BUILT 1926)
BUS GARAGE ADDED 1933

Former Horse Car Depot

Original layout, all removed by 1915

① BELGRAVE
② MELTON ROAD

Auth'd extn to city boundary. 0.5 miles from Y
Auth'd extn to city boundary. 0.7 miles from X

To Anstey, Groby & Newtown Linford

Leicester, Anstey, Groby & Newtown Linford Light Railway (authorised route)

Passengers until 1928. Freight until 1966.

Original course at Groby Road

Overhead wiring removed ca. 1924

⑨ GROBY ROAD
① WESTERN PARK
③ ④ FOSSE ROAD

① BELGRAVE
② MELTON ROAD

curve removed 1924

Belgrave Road Station until 1930

Abbey Park Rd. Depot & Works
Power Station

BELGRAVE ROAD STATION
RUSSELL SQUARE

HUMBERSTONE
⑦ HUMBERSTONE
⑧ COLEMAN ROAD

HUMBERSTONE STATION

Spinney Hills

① EAST PARK ROAD
②
④ MELBOURNE ROAD

HUMBERSTONE ROAD STN.

MELBOURNE ROAD

LONDON ROAD STATION

WEST BRIDGE STN.

FROG ISLAND
WOOD GATE

Evington Drive

WELFORD ROAD

© R.A.Smith, January 2007.
Amended March 2023. No. 769 v.1.4
Based on J.C.Gillham's Map No.85
(after K.W.Smith) dated August 1930,
as revised (after M.S.W.Pearson)

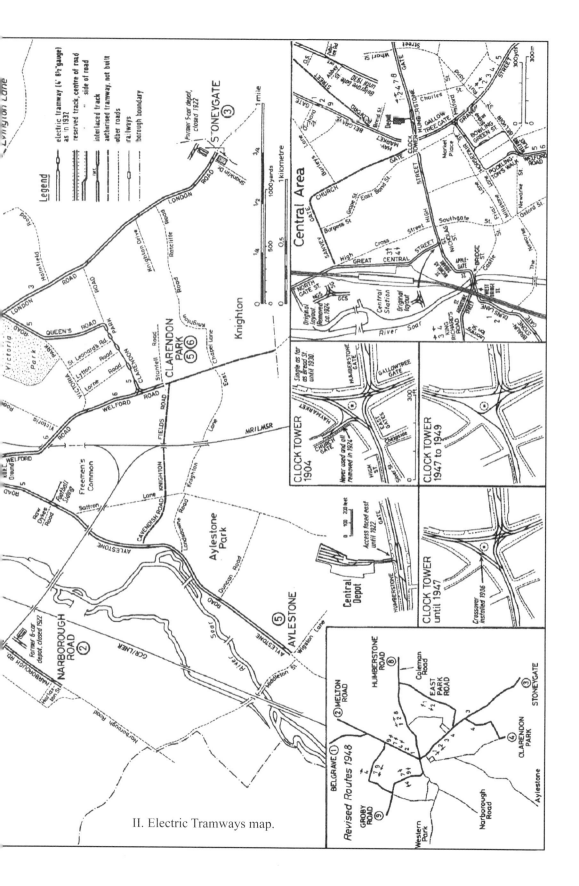

II. Electric Tramways map.

HORSE BUSES

1. Horse bus 4 of the Leicester Tramways Company is seen at what is thought to be Park Vale Road, adjacent to Spinney Hill Park, circa 1900; the slip board below the central windows is advertising a service to Saxe-Coburg Street and Park Vale. The former road was re-named Saxby Street due to First World War Germanic sensitivities. The stern looking gentlemen on the top deck looks towards the photographer above an advertisement for knife polish. The pipe-smoking conductor in the foreground is Mr Jesse A. Walters. Note the brake block on the rear wheel.
(A.P. Newland collection/
Leicester Transport Heritage Trust)

➔   2. A horse bus service from Knighton Road to Oadby village was operating by July 1878. The company obtained powers to lay a tramway from Stoneygate to Oadby church, but this was never built. Instead, the company introduced a horse bus service to the Black Dog Hotel in the village. In this picture, the horses take their refreshment from the nose bags containing hay or chaff; in this picture the bus is now in the ownership of Leicester Corporation. The Seabreeze advertisement was for a salt drink, which was recommended to be taken warm in cold weather. The Black Dog hotel still exists, and has a history going back to 1750 as a coaching inn. The building on the right has been replaced with a modern structure housing the hotel's function room and skittle alley. (Leicester Transport Heritage Trust)

HORSE TRAMS

3.   The first horse tram service was opened on 24rd December 1874 from the Clock Tower to the Folly Inn, Belgrave. Single deck Car 9 is illustrated here at the Groby Road terminus in 1902, with the crew posing for the photographer, and a lone female passenger seated behind. The original cars were single deck, and some were converted to double deck with upper deck fitted with back-to-back knifeboard seating. Car 9 retained its single deck status. (Author's collection)

4.   Double deck Car 2 enters single track in Humberstone Gate circa 1890, possibly in a red and white livery. In 1885, a new depot was opened by the tramway company in Belgrave Gate, replacing earlier facilities in the same thoroughfare; the former included a manager's house and stables for 80 horses. Bass Burton ales were sold in The Tower Vaults public house on the left; earlier names for the property were The Barrel and Rhine Wine Vaults.
(Leicester Transport Heritage Trust)

5.   Car 27 is seen here in London Road circa 1899, with the driver clutching the hand brake handle. The two horses are wearing head apparel secured over their ears; the purpose is unclear, unless it is to provide protection from the sun. This is the only image seen with this item of equipment. Note what appears to be a steel telegraph pole to the rear. (Leicester Transport Heritage Trust)

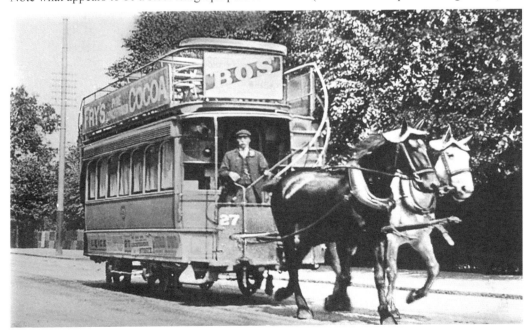

6. Car 15, destined to provide walking access to Melbourne Hall in St Peters Road, climbs the hill in London Road circa 1903 with the aid of a third trace, or cock, horse to assist with the incline. On reaching the top, the third horse will be detached to make its way down hill to assist with the next car. The top deck passengers appear to be enjoying the sunny weather. The Hall now houses the Evangelical Free Church.
(Leicester Transport Heritage Trust)

III. A 25ins to 1 mile map of central Leicester pre 1904 showing the horse tram track.

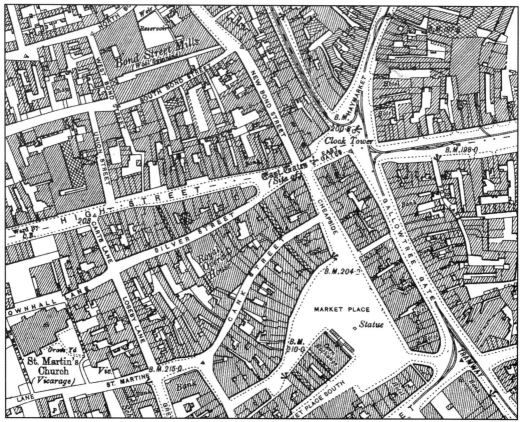

7. Car 18 stands at the Belgrave terminus in May 1904, with Thurcaston Road on the left, and the local school, which is now a solicitor's practice, as the backdrop. Track can be seen leading into Thurcaston Road, which led to a horse tram depot a short distance from the junction. (Leicester Transport Heritage Trust)

SERVICE NUMBERS

During the period of electric tram operation, there were many variations in the linking of the various cross-town services, particularly towards the system closure. It is beyond the scope of this publication to list all these variations, but below is a list of the service numbers when they were fully introduced in 1933, and as indicated on the maps.

1	East Park Road - Humberstone Road - Western Park - Belgrave
2	East Park Road - London Road - Narborough Road - Melton Road
3	Stoneygate - Fosse Road (via Great Central Street)
4	Melbourne Road - Fosse Road (via King Richard's Road)
5	Clarendon Park - Town Hall - Aylestone
6	Town Hall - Clarendon Park (via Welford Road)
7	Clock Tower - Humberstone
8	Clock Tower - Coleman Road
9	Belgrave Road/Abby Park Road junction - Groby Road (via Abbey Park Road and Blackbird Road)
12	Special Duties

ELECTRIC TRAMS

Clock Tower

8. Open top Car 30 is about to leave the Clock Tower to enter Haymarket en route to Belgrave, with the Leicester Coffee House building, which still exists, in the background to the right; a modern equivalent of the latter is in Granby Street. Beyond the Clock Tower is the Clothing Hall, which announces it caters for 'all classes', indicating the British class system was alive and well. The roads are remarkably clear of horse droppings, perhaps due in some part to the gentleman with his broom and tray; this area, and the adjacent streets other than Church Gate, are now pedestrianised. Note the exterior lights which shine into the window displays of the shops on the right.
(Commercial postcard/
Author's collection)

9.   In August 1946, Car 131 passes through the Clock Tower area en route to Clarendon Park, with the large Bovril advertisement prominent. Below, there are advertisements for Picture Post, a highly regarded photographic magazine, which was published between 1938 and 1957, and Lilliput, a publication comprising mainly of humour, short stories, photographs and art content. It was first published in 1937, and was absorbed into a sister magazine in 1960.
(M.J. O'Connor/National Tramway Museum)

➔   10.   Looking towards the Clock Tower from High Street and East Gates in May 1937, the decorations are out to celebrate the coronation of King George VI and Queen Elizabeth. Car 111 is about to turn right into Gallowtree Gate and onwards to Stoneygate, as Car 41 leaves the Clock Tower to continue along High Street to Fosse Road; both cars are decorated, as were the rest of the vehicles in service. The four-storey building to the right of 41 still exists, and houses a Virgin Media store. The period road sign on the left indicates a gyratory system around the Clock Tower, but this did not apply to the trams until June 1947. In the foreground, a pedestrian crosses between the studded corridor identified by the Belisha beacon adjacent to the road sign; black and white road stripes only appeared post war.
(S.G. Jackman)

↓ 11. Balcony Car 121 turns out of East Gates to enter Gallowtree Gate on service to Stoneygate, circa 1907, as an open top car moves in the opposite direction past The Coffee House. Inspectors wait to talk to 121's motorman as pedestrians wander across the tram tracks.
(A.P. Newland collection/Leicester Transport Heritage Trust)

12. The major civil engineering work to install tram track around the Clock Tower is almost complete, which was reported as being the most complex in the United Kingdom. Working round in a clockwise direction, at the top right of the picture is East Gates, leading into High Street, with Church Gate to the right. The latter, used by horse trams, comprised a short dead-end length of track, which was never used by electric trams, and removed in 1924. Haymarket, leading in to Belgrave Gate, is to the rear of the photographer, and Humberstone Gate plus Gallowtree Gate are on the extreme left. The two buildings in the right-hand distance, on the corner of Cheapside, still exist. (Leicester Transport Heritage Trust)

➔ *Electrical supply cabinet.*

13. With Coronation decorations adorning the surrounding buildings, Car 32 makes its way south through Haymarket on Service 1 past the White Hart Hotel, demolished to make way for the Haymarket Shopping Centre, and onwards to East Park Road in May 1937. Alexandre, the men's outfitters, is next to the hotel entrance; this was the company from which the author purchased his first teenage suit in Derby. The between decks advertisement is exhorting Leicester citizens to support the purchase of Canadian produce. Note the extremely long extension ladder to the rear. (S. Newton)

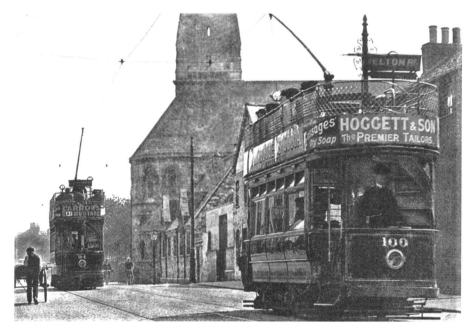

↑ 14. St Mark's church dominates this photograph, taken in 1911, with open top Car 100 (formerly 137) travelling north along Belgrave Gate, now a dual carriageway, en route to Melton Road; similar Car 34 moves in the opposite direction towards the Clock Tower. The church opened in 1870, and in 2005 changed its role from a place of religious worship to a banqueting and conference centre named 'The Empire'. (W.H. Stone)

← 15.   A circa 1918 view looking north along Belgrave Gate, a short distance from the Clock Tower, with the Palace Theatre opposite Car 132, now fitted with a top cover whilst retaining open balconies. The theatre was opened in 1901, and seated 3,500, claiming to be the largest establishment outside of London. It became a film cinema in the periods 1931 to 1937, and 1938 to 1946, before returning as a theatre. It closed in 1959, and was subsequently demolished. The premises of Billson and Son appeared to specialise in the supply of outdoor equipment, including tents, marquees, ropes etc.
(Commercial postcard/
A.P. Newland collection)

16.   Where Belgrave Gate becomes Belgrave Road, Car 92 travels south past the Belgrave Road railway station, adjacent to the current traffic island, on Service 2 to East Park Road circa 1939. The station was opened in 1883 by the Great Northern Railway to provide an easterly line to Peterborough and Grantham, thereby making a connection to London Kings Cross and the north east. It also provided many summertime holiday specials to the east coast seaside resorts. Patronage declined in the 1950s and the line was closed in 1962, although for a period, a connection was made with the Midland main line to serve several commercial depots. The rear of a Leicester Guy CX 3-axle motorbus can be seen beyond 92.
(A.P. Newland collection)

Outwards towards Melton Road and Belgrave

17. A busy post war scene with Car 2 on Service 3 travelling south along Belgrave Road, and approaching the junction with Abbey Park Road on the left. The property on the corner was occupied by T.E. Cundy and Son who owned a decorating business, and the building has been replaced with a more modern structure housing a Turkish restaurant, which also encompasses the site of the first demolished gable ended building; the buildings beyond all still exist. An Austin car, registered in 1947, approaches the photographer as many cyclists occupy the road space.
(F.N.T. Lloyd-Jones/Online Transport Archive)

BELGRAVE & MELTON ROAD SERVICES

Belgrave Tramcars from either terminus every 3, 3½, 4, 4½, 5 and 6 minutes.

	Weekdays.	Saturdays.	Sundays.
First Car—Clock Tower ..	6.10 a.m.	6.10 a.m.	9.38 a.m.
,, ,, Terminus ..	6.26½ a.m.	6.26½ a.m.	9.37 a.m.
Last Car—Clock Tower ..	11. 0 p.m.	11.16 p.m.	10.48 p.m.
,, ,, Terminus ..	11.14 p.m.	11.30 p.m.	11. 1 p.m.

Melton Road Tramcars from either Terminus every 3, 3½, 4, 4½, 5 and 6 minutes.

	Weekdays.	Saturdays.	Sundays.
First Car—Clock Tower ..	6.15 a.m.	6.15 a.m.	9.40½ a.m.
,, ,, Terminus ..	6.29 a.m.	6.29 a.m.	9.40½ a.m.
Last Car—Clock Tower ..	11.2½ p.m.	11.18 p.m.	10.46 p.m.
,, ,, Terminus ..	11.17½ p.m.	11.33 p.m.	11. 0 p.m.

18. Car 6 has just left the Loughborough Road/Melton Road junction in the distance, and is heading south past the Cooper Street short working facility, where the triangular overhead wiring for the boom reversal can be seen on the right. The areas beyond the hoardings have been redeveloped; one advertisement is for the Theatre Royal, which opened in 1836 and was demolished in 1958. Note the roundabout road sign on the left-hand traction standard, which did not apply to the trams. (F.N.T. Lloyd-Jones/Online Transport Archive)

19. Car 118 heading north has reached the Loughborough Road/Melton Road junction, and is about to turn left into the former on Service 1 to Belgrave in September 1949. On the left, a coach belonging to Allen's of Mountsorrel travels in the opposite direction, whilst in the distance on the right a post war Midland Red underfloor engine single deck bus can be seen. (W.A. Camwell/National Tramway Museum)

20.   Car 40 moves north along Melton Road past the Jermyn Street short working facility on Service 2 to Melton Road circa 1941. The picture illustrates wartime blackout precautions with Car 40 fitted with a masked headlight and white painted bumper and lifeguard, plus the black and white bands painted on the traction standards to help traffic in the wartime blackout. Note what appears to be a cigarette dispensing machine on the left.
(A.P. Newland collection/Leicester Transport Heritage Trust)

21.   Car 155 has just left the Melton Road terminus in September 1938 and is destined for East Park Road via the Clock Tower, with a second tram standing at the end of the track ready to use the crossover to return to the city centre. The front of the shop on the corner of Stafford Street has been extended to incorporate the bay window and now sells luggage items.
(W.A. Camwell/National Tramway Museum)

22. With the Premier Works of T.G. Hunt & Son, who were boot manufacturers, as the backdrop, the motorman of Car 2 looks towards the photographer at the Melton Road terminus as he takes a break before returning to East Park Road, circa 1949. The site is now occupied by a Morrisons store and filling station. Car 2 was rebuilt in the 1930s with extended frames and platforms.
(F.E.J. Ward/Online Transport Archive)

→ *Second World War II poster warning drivers to avoid arcing.*

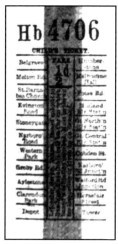

23. On the opposite side of the road from the previous picture, Haley's Garage provides the background for Car 110 waiting to reverse for a return to East Park Road. There are three Esso branded petrol pumps, plus one carrying the Shell logo lamp cover, with the gentleman in the trilby hat smoking a cigarette; so much for health and safety! The site is now occupied by the Green Motion car and van rental company. Note the concrete telephone box beyond, and the current Rushey Fields Recreation Grounds.
(F.N.T. Lloyd-Jones/
Online Transport Archive)

24. Car 129 returning from Belgrave, leaves Loughborough Road to join Belgrave Road and onwards to Stoneygate in May 1949. A Foden lorry follows close behind and the properties to the rear still exist, although their occupancy has changed over the years. By the time this photograph was taken, trams no longer served Melton Road, with the overhead wiring removed and tied off as can be seen top right. 129 carries an advertisement for the Everybody's tabloid magazine, which was founded in 1913, and ceased publication in 1959. (R.B. Parr/National Tramway Museum)

25. An early 1949 view at the same location as the previous picture depicts Car 130 destined for Stoneygate. A Brown's Blue utility Bedford bus enters the picture from the left, and a Southdown Leyland coach, well away from its south coast operating area, waits to join Melton Road. Note how the traffic on the left negotiates the small traffic island, which 130 has avoided.
(F.N.T. Lloyd-Jones/Online Transport Archive)

26. Car 123 moves along Loughborough Road and is about to pass the end of Thurcaston Road on the left, with a second car in the distance near the Belgrave terminus. This location was the site of the terminus for the horse tram service to Belgrave; a horse tram depot was located in Thurcaston Road, which had been removed by 1915. The school is now a solicitors' practice, and the junction controlled by traffic lights. Note the iconic Bovril advertisement on the end of the building, which still exists. (F.N.T. Lloyd-Jones/Online Transport Archive)

→ 27. Three cars stand at the Belgrave terminus on what appears to be a warm day in August 1947. In the foreground, Car 118 waits to return to East Park Road on Service 1, and immediately behind is Car 86 on an enthusiasts' special, which would be displaying Service 12 used for such special duties. At the rear is a service car with boom fully extended under the boom reversing wiring. The Brayshaw and Carr garage is on the right. (J.E. Gready)

← *Boom reversal wiring.*

↓   28.   Looking in the opposite direction, circa September 1947, both cars have completed the reversing manoeuvre with the boom of Car 83 just about to join the wiring back to the city centre. The garage forecourt is in a very tidy condition with three pumps and an airline, plus an Austin saloon; the site is now occupied by a Lidl store. (F.E.J. Ward/Online Transport Archive)

Outwards to Groby Road

29. Having left Belgrave Road, and travelling in a westerly direction, Car 136 crosses the bridge in Abbey Park Road over what was known as the Leicester Canal which runs north to south, with connections with the River Soar at each end; it is now classed as part of the Grand Union Canal. On the bridge wall the words 'Static Water' can be seen indicating an emergency water supply, which would have been handy in the event of fire during the Second World War. On the left are the original Abbey Park Mills owned by Wolsey Limited, a hosiery manufacturer, now being converted into accommodation by several agencies. In front of the building are the track and overhead wiring leading into the Abbey Park Road depot. To the rear is one of the AEC Renown 3-axle motorbuses specified by the pre-war General Manager to instigate the tram replacement programme, plus a Fordson articulated lorry with low load trailer. (F.N.T. Lloyd-Jones/Online Transport Archive)

BLACKBIRD ROAD AND GROBY ROAD

is an outer route that skirts the north-west side of the City between Belgrave Road and Fosse Road (North).

Blackbird and Groby Roads Tramcars from either terminus every 10, 15 and 30 minutes at certain periods of the day.

	Weekdays.	Saturdays.	Sundays.
First Car—Abbey Park Road	6.55 a.m.	6.55 a.m.	10.30 a.m.
,, ,, Groby Road ..	7.10 a.m.	7.10 a.m.	10.45½ a.m.
Last Car—Abbey Park Road	11. 0 p.m.	11. 0 p.m.	10. 0 p.m.
,, ,, Groby Road ..	11.15 p.m.	11.15 p.m.	10.15 p.m.

On Sundays, a Service also operates between **Groby Road Terminus** and **Clock Tower**, *via* Sanvey Gate as follows :—

First Car—Clock Tower	..	1.20 p.m.
,, ,, Groby Road	..	1.45 p.m.
Last Car—Clock Tower	..	5.20 p.m.
,, ,, Groby Road	..	5.42 p.m.

30. The main access to the Abbey Park Road Depot and Works provides the backdrop as Car 38 moves in an easterly direction towards Belgrave Road, circa February 1949. The enclosure on the top of the office block is possibly a wartime fire watch station and/or enemy aircraft recognition site. In the background is the erstwhile factory of Gipsy Queen, a brand that still exists, manufacturers of female fashion footwear. All the buildings have disappeared, and the entrance to Abbey Park is on the left. (F.N.T. Lloyd-Jones/Online Transport Archive)

31. Further along Abbey Park Road towards Blackbird Road, Car 160 is about to cross the bridge over the River Soar whilst travelling east towards Belgrave Road. The factory in the background, known as Abbey Meadow Mills, was also owned by Wolsey Limited, which has been converted into luxury apartments. To the left, a short distance along the river bank, are the National Space Centre and the Abbey Pumping Station Museum of Science and Technology.
(F.N.T. Lloyd-Jones/Online Transport Archive)

32. Car 173 has reached the northern end of the reserved central reservation track in Blackbird Road, and waits by the time clock next to the rear platform before turning right under the railway bridge to reach Abbey Park Road. Esso oil tank wagons can be seen on the ex-London North Eastern Railway (Great Central Railway) track, which at the time the photograph was taken had become British Railways as a result of the Labour Government's post war nationalisation programme. Advertising boards adorn the wall under the bridge, which no longer exists, with the steelwork carrying an advert for Leicester Co-op bread; the area to the left is now occupied by an industrial estate.
(F.N.T. Lloyd-Jones/Online Transport Archive)

→ 33. Car 59 has reached Groby Road Corner, having travelled from the named terminus in June 1937, and will now move forward to turn left into Blackbird Road; this four-way junction is now controlled by traffic lights. The white band on the traction standard signifies a tram stop. The track in the foreground curving to the right into Fosse Road North remains, although the overhead wiring was removed circa 1924. This was the location of one of the five art deco passenger shelters; note that the hardware shop on the left has a fine display of deck chairs.
(H.B. Priestley/National Tramway Museum)

↓   34. At the Groby Road terminus, which was close to Brading Road on the left, Car 62 has crossed over to the inward bound track in June 1948. Where 62 stands was the original alignment of Groby Road before being re-aligned to the left in 1935 to remove a sharp bend. (J.H. Meredith/Online Transport Archive)

35. Cars 58 and 116 stand in Humberstone Gate opposite the Stag and Pheasant Hotel. 116 is destined for Stoneygate on Service 3, as passengers disembark into the roadway. 58 is on Service 4 to Clarendon Park. By the late 1700s, the hotel had become a premier coaching inn, in addition to providing for Royal Mail coaches. The premises closed in 1959, and the building was subsequently demolished to make way for the Haymarket Shopping Centre. The Maconachie company advertises its soups on the left-hand building; the company's stew did not find favour with front line troops in the Boer and 1914-18 wars.
(F.N.T. Lloyd-Jones/Online Transport Archive)

36.   At the same location, with the hotel on the right, Car 62 awaits departure to Humberstone on Service 8. This service number was used after the Coleman Road service ceased in October 1938. The Burton's store is on the opposite corner, and beyond is Edmonds wool shop, plus the premises of Dean and Dawson who were agents for the London Midland and Scottish Railway. The car parked on the right is a 1935 American Plymouth saloon, as a post war Leicester motorbus pulls in behind 62. (F.N.T. Lloyd-Jones/Online Transport Archive)

Historical plaque.

*Notice of two minutes' silence for the funeral
of King George V in January 1936.*

37. In the wide expanse of Humberstone Gate, we see Car 28 on Service 1 to Western Park, and Car 132 destined for East Park Road on Service 2 in June 1937. The gap between 28 and the parked car is too narrow for the Armstrong Siddeley car behind to overtake, so the driver waits for the tram to move forward. On the opposite side of the road, adjacent to 132, is the Admiral Nelson public house which dates back to the early 1800s. It was sold to the council in 1972, and subsequently demolished to make way for the Haymarket Shopping Centre.
(H.B. Priestley/National Tramway Museum)

38. Car 7 waits at the central dead-end stand for Service 8 to Humberstone (see earlier caption regarding service number). The rear bus on the left is 334, a 3 axle AEC Renown from 1940, whilst in front is 65, an AEC Regent lll, with locally built Brush bodywork delivered in 1949. To the left of both is the original John Lewis store, which was demolished in the 1990s, apart from the tower, which remains. The passenger shelter to the rear of Car 7 was in position by early 1924.
(F.N.T. Lloyd-Jones/Online Transport Archive)

39. At the same location, Car 88 waits before leaving on Service 7, the original service number, to Humberstone in July 1938. Also in view is Car 47 on Service 4, and in the distance Car 84 on Service 2 to East Park Road; the latter two trams appear to be on the same track, but travelling in opposite directions. 47 is in the new livery, but 88 would never be so treated being withdrawn in 1939. (W.A. Camwell/National Tramway Museum)

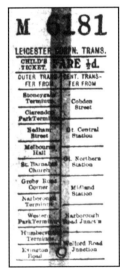

40. Also at the same location, but seen from the opposite side, this poor wartime image depicts the conductress of Car 31 posing for an American serviceman photographer. The photograph was taken in May 1943, and the photographer went on to take several other tram views while he was in the city. 31 is fitted with a masked headlight, plus a white painted bumper to help others in the wartime blackout. (G.F. Cunningham/
National Tramway Museum)

41. Car 83 crosses between tracks in June 1948, with the boom at full stretch on overhead wiring that was positioned to allow boom reversal on the forward movement of the tram, thereby not requiring conductor assistance. To the right is Car 138 with two other cars beyond, plus a pre-war Leyland motorbus. On the extreme left is the Admiral Nelson pub, with The Plough public house next door; both made way for the Haymarket Shopping Centre.
(R.F. Mack)

42. The old order changeth. A busy scene taken in September 1949 depicts the old in the form of Cars 62 and 138, both showing Service 8, and the new depicted by the two post war motorbuses on the right. In the foreground is AEC Regent III (54) fitted with Brush bodywork on Service 33 to East Park Road, and an all Leyland PD2 (103) product behind being overtaken by a Commer van. The delivery of these vehicles, plus the training of drivers, allowed the conversion programme to be brought forward by two years.
(W.A. Camwell/National Tramway Museum)

43. With the impressive St Luke's church as the backdrop, Car 72 rounds the bend in Humberstone Road adjacent to Bell Lane whilst on Service 8 circa February 1949; the church was demolished in 1950. In the foreground is a wartime Bedford lorry, where the pre-war design of the bonnet and radiator areas has changed to the simpler rectangular design depicted incorporating a crash bar. On the left is the sign for the London North Western Vaults, originally known as the Humberstone Tavern; the pub closed in 1957. The former name probably reflected the nearby railway goods yard and warehouse; the latter can be seen to the right the church.
(F.N.T. Lloyd-Jones/Online Transport Archive)

44. Moving further east along Humberstone Road in September 1949, Car 7 passes under the bridge carrying the ex-London Midland and Scottish Railway (Midland Railway) line from London St Pancras to Nottingham, Derby and Sheffield whilst returning to the city centre. Beyond the semaphore signals is Humberstone Road Station, which closed in 1968. Although difficult to discern, the overhead wiring has been slewed to one side of the track alignment to provide adequate clearance for trams passing under the structure. Note the number of cyclists, and the bridge advertisement for Morris cars. (W.A. Camwell/National Tramway Museum)

→ 45. Car 80 is on Uppingham Road having just passed Saint Barnabas Road on the right in September 1949, which was used by the East Park Road circular services. A bus and Ford Popular have overtaken, and approach the ex-London North Eastern Railway (Great Northern Railway) bridge carrying the line from the east into Leicester. Note the advertisement for the Co-operative Wholesale Society, which was a federation where consumer co-operatives could collectively purchase goods at wholesale prices and, in some cases, collectively own factories or farms. (W.A. Camwell/National Tramway Museum)

→ 46. Car 117 passes under the same bridge in Uppingham Road, which carried the railway line to the right into the ex-London North Eastern Railway (Great Northern Railway) Belgrave Road station, with Humberstone station and signal box above the right-hand embankment; this station was closed in 1962. The line in the opposite easterly direction ensured Grantham, Peterborough and beyond could be reached. It looks as if the road under the bridge has been lowered to give adequate tram clearance. Following close behind is a Midland Red FEDD double deck front entrance motorbus, in an otherwise deserted road. (F.N.T. Lloyd-Jones/Online Transport Archive)

47. On a wet day, Car 45 waits next to the time clock at the Humberstone terminus on the last day of tram operation in the city on 9th November 1949. Between the two is a police box, complete with blue light above the door, presumably with a policeman inside judging by the parked bicycle. Note that telegraph poles were still being used in 1949. (R.E. Tustin)

48. Looking in the opposite direction, Car 6 in the background has reached the end of the track at the Humberstone Drive terminus, whilst Car 1 has used the crossover ready to return to the city centre. Beyond 6 is the Trocadero cinema, which was opened in 1931, and destroyed by fire in 1967. To the right is one of five art deco passenger shelters gifted to the city by Robert Rowley in 1934, a local knitwear and hosiery manufacturer, and designed by local architect Waller King Bedingfield. One was also built in Western Boulevard for the county bound bus services terminating in that area. Beyond the shelter on the right is Humberstone Park, which was opened in 1925, having previously been a private estate. Note the period road sign on the left. (F.E.J. Ward/Online Transport Archive)

49. This is the point where the Coleman Road service left Uppingham Road, with Car 125 destined for Groby Road about to leave the former in 1938. The Coleman Road service was the last section of tramway to be built, which opened on 31st March 1927. The building housing the corner grocery store still exists, but is now occupied by a Papa John pizza outlet. The car behind is an early 1930s Vauxhall Cadet saloon. (S. Newton)

HUMBERSTONE AND COLEMAN ROAD SERVICES

Humberstone Tramcars from either terminus every 4 and 5½ minutes.

	Weekdays.	Saturdays.	Sundays.
First Car—Clock Tower ..	6. 5 a.m.	6. 5 a.m.	9.39 a.m.
,, ,, Terminus ..	6.21 a.m.	6.21 a.m.	9.55 a.m.
Last Car—Clock Tower ..	11. 3 p.m.	11.19½ p.m.	10.45½ p.m.
,, ,, Terminus ..	11.19 p.m.	11.35½ p.m.	11.1½ p.m.

Coleman Road Tramcars from either terminus every 11 and 16 minutes.

First Car—Clock Tower ..	6.22 a.m.	6.22 a.m.	9.42 a.m.
,, ,, Terminus ..	6.39 a.m.	6.39 a.m.	9.58 a.m.
Last Car—Clock Tower ..	11. 0 p.m.	11.17 p.m.	10.46 p.m.
,, ,, Terminus ..	11.17 p.m.	11.34 p.m.	11. 2 p.m.

50. The Coleman Road service comprised a mixture of single track with passing loops, plus reserved track on the final stretch to the terminus. Here we see Car 47 on this last section moving towards the terminus in September 1938; the service closed on 23rd October 1938. The development of local authority housing stock in the area led to the service's early demise, with motorbuses providing an extended replacement service. 47 is in the 1937 livery with a cream band at the base of the lower panels, plus the platform aprons; this feature was dispensed with after the Second Word War.
(Leicester Evening Mail/
P. Hollins collection)

51. Car 115 has reached the end of the line at Green Lane Road, and waits on the short length of double track before returning from Coleman Road to Groby Road sometime between September 1937 and the service closure. The passenger shelter on the right was converted from the body of a single deck bus, and the scene is illuminated in the hours of darkness by the floodlight mounted on the cantilevered bracket arm; the box attached to the traction standard contained an emergency telephone. Beyond is space for a proposed tramway extension along Broad Avenue towards the General Hospital. The circular structure on the right is the sign for the Full Moon Hotel located on the corner of Green Lane Road, with the moon being the central circular feature.
(S. Newton)

Melbourne Road

52. Looking back along the length of Melbourne Road circa 1907, open top Car 46 approaches a passing loop, with the Grade II listed Melbourne Hall on the right; on entering the loop, 46 will immediately turn to its right into St Peter's Road. The building was completed in 1881 as a Baptist church, and is now occupied by the Evangelical Free Church. This service provided an inner link between Humberstone and London Roads, and comprised single track and passing loops. It was closed in December 1933. (Commercial postcard/A.P. Newland collection)

EAST PARK ROAD SERVICE

East Park Road Tramcars from Clock Tower either way every 3, 3½, 4, 4½, 5 and 6 minutes. (Circular Route).

	Weekdays.	Saturdays.	Sundays.
First Car—East Park *via*			
London Road	6.15 a.m.	6.15 a.m.	9.41 a.m.
,, ,, East Park *via*			
Humberstone Rd.	6.10 a.m.	6.10 a.m.	9.38½ a.m.
Last Car—East Park *via*			
London Road ..	11. 3 p.m.	11.17 p.m.	10.47 p.m.
,, ,, East Park *via*			
Humberstone Rd.	11.0½ p.m.	11.15 p.m.	10.45 p.m.

East Park Road Circulars

The anti-clockwise route operated as Service 1, outward via London Road and returning to the city centre via Humberstone Road. The clockwise route was Service 2, and operated in the opposite direction. Having crossed the city centre, the services travelled onwards to Belgrave and Melton Road respectively.

53. On an anti-clockwise circuit, Car 153 has just passed the junction with Green Lane Road and is about to enter St Barnabas Road, travelling onwards to Uppingham Road. Originally this length of track comprised a single line with passing loops, and a short working crossover, which can be seen immediately behind 153. All the property that can be seen still exists, other than the building to the left of 153; the tall building on the right houses the Nexus bathroom and kitchen showrooms. Note the pedestrian crossing identified by the metal studs in the road surface.
(F.N.T. Lloyd-Jones/Online Transport Archive)

54. Car 150 travels along East Park Road on a clockwise circuit, having just passed St Saviours Road on the right; the parish church of St Stephen's is just out of view on the right. The only other traffic is in the far distance, and all the buildings still exist; the Midland Bank building is now occupied by Deepa's, a women's fashion store. (F.N.T. Lloyd-Jones/Online Transport Archive)

55. Car 123, destined for Melton Road, climbs the incline on East Park Road on a clockwise circuit past the end of Cork Street on the left, with Spinney Hill Park in the distance. The ground floors of the two properties on the left have been converted to accommodate the Cloud 9 Desserts business. A Ford car is parked next to the bicycle on the left. (F.N.T. Lloyd-Jones/Online Transport Archive)

56.   Cars 25 and 26 pass on their respective circuits at the junction of East Park Road and Chesterfield Road, which is on the right. The domed building on the right once housed the Evington Cinema, and the façade, now known as Fara House, is occupied by a solicitors' practice. Car 26 is showing Service 3 to Stoneygate via Humberstone and London Roads; this service variant was introduced on 7th July 1947 following the closure of the Fosse Road service, and lasted until 15th May 1949. (R.S.J. Wiseman/National Tramway Museum)

57.   The tram tracks have now left East Park Road with a turn into Evington Road, and here we see Car 78 in the foreground moving along the latter past the Barclays Bank on the corner of St Stephen's Road. The building has been modernised, although the branch is currently closed. Both cars are in a passing loop, which was a feature of this stretch of road, and are about to enter a single section of track. (F.N.T. Lloyd-Jones/Online Transport Archive)

58. Further along Evington Road, Car 78 rounds the bend adjacent to Abingdon Road on an anti-clockwise circuit and is about to leave a passing loop; if there were to be trams on either side of the loop, there would be insufficient space for others to pass. Tracks in the opposite clockwise direction eventually join London Road, and onwards into the city centre. The lady in the foreground steps out complete with what appears to be a fox fur. (F.N.T. Lloyd-Jones/Online Transport Archive)

59. This mid-afternoon picture has Car 74, destined for Narborough Road circa 1948, leaving single track at the end of Evington Road where the double tracks will immediately join those in London Road. All the buildings on the left have disappeared, apart from a lone derelict takeaway shop. (A.P. Newland collection)

Gallowtree Gate

60. With the Clock Tower in the distance, Car 156 passes the end of Horsefair Street in Gallowtree Gate whilst on Service 1 to East Park Road. The traction standard carries a tram stop and a 'No Waiting' sign for the period 10.30am to 4.00pm. Work is in hand on the shop fronts in the foreground, and next door is a branch of Spalls, a gift shop, who also had a branch in Derby. (F.N.T. Lloyd-Jones/Online Transport Archive)

61. On what appears to be a very wet day in 1948, Car 63 turns out of Humberstone Gate around Burton's corner, currently a large HSBC bank, into Gallowtree Gate. The weather does not seem to have put off the throngs of shoppers. Most of the females are wearing head scarves, not a fashion statement seen in today's street scene. (Leicester Mercury/P. Hollins collection)

62. This late afternoon picture, taken in September 1949, looks along the length of Gallowtree Gate from the Clock Tower. Car 118 follows a Carter Paterson/Pickfords wartime Bedford OL parcels delivery van, with the driver positioning his hand for a possible hand signal to turn right. This joint parcel company was absorbed into British Road Services following the nationalisation of the road haulage industry by the post war Labour Government. Today, a modern H. Samuel shop is in the same right-hand location depicted here, complete with clock, which is now in a lower position. (W.A. Camwell/National Tramway Museum)

Driver and conductor tokens.

63. Looking towards the Clock Tower, balcony Car 102 moves south along Gallowtree Gate past the junction with Horsefair Street on the left circa 1906. Horse drawn carts are part of the street scene, and the building on the right houses the district office of the Royal Liver Friendly Society, who created the world-famous Royal Liver Building at Liverpool's Pier Head. The corner building on the left still exists, but those to the right have made way for more modern structures. (Commercial postcard/A.P. Newland collection)

64. At the same location, open top Cars 26 and 8 are seen in Gallowtree Gate circa 1906 at the junction with Horsefair Street on the left, and travelling in opposite directions on the circular services to Melbourne Road, which were discontinued in 1933. A three-wheeled pedal basket barrow can be seen on the right, and the Sanito Toilet Saloon is on the opposite side of the road, where a shave cost 2d. An advertisement for the Palace Theatre, which provided twice nightly shows, is sited above the Friendly Society signage. (Commercial postcard/Author's collection)

← 65. The importance of trams transporting the citizens of Leicester immediately after the Second World War, and before widespread car ownership, is illustrated in this Saturday July 1947 scene. There are seven trams in this view along Gallowtree Gate; Cars 39 and 51 are in the foreground, and will turn left into East Gates on reaching the Clock Tower to reach their loading stands in High Street.
(A.P. Newland collection/
Leicester Transport Heritage Trust)

Granby Street

66. Car 79, on Service 1 to Belgrave, leaves Granby Street in early 1949, and is about to enter Gallowtree Gate past the policeman standing on a wooden box directing traffic. The sign on the box side reads, 'Wait for the policeman's signal'. A horse and cart disappear into Halford Street on the left, and opposite, tracks curve round into Horsefair Street. The premises of Dunn and Company, a hat makers that also sold men's formal wear, is seen on the left-hand corner. The decline in the use of hats in the second half of the 20th century, and the advent of new High Street retailers, led to the company's demise.
(F.E.J. Ward/Online Transport Archive)

67. Car 136 has reached the Rutland Street/Belvoir Street junction, and passes the Wellington Commercial Hotel whilst on Service 1 to East Park Road; the lower hotel floor is now occupied by a Tesco Express. Beyond 136 is the Grade II listed Victoria Coffee House, formally the Temperance Coffee House built in 1888, which, together with similar establishments in the city, was the initiative of the temperance movement to reduce drunkenness in the city.
(F.N.T. Lloyd-Jones/Online Transport Archive)

68. Having crossed the junction seen in the last picture, Car 26 continues along Granby Street past the Grand Hotel en route to Melbourne Road, with shrubbery installed above the hotel entrance. A lone horse is being led in the opposite direction and, on the left, the large model spectacles indicate the premises of an optician, with a window cleaner and his barrow outside. Beyond 26 is the Jays store, which had a restaurant on the top floor. (Commercial postcard/Author's collection)

69. Travelling in the opposite direction past the hotel entrance, Car 90 is destined for Uppingham Road. The boys and girls look towards the photographer, with one of the former wearing an apron, and carrying a delivery basket. The hotel is Grade II listed, and was built in 1897-98; the Kings Hall area of the building was once a cinema, and the hotel is currently operated by Mercure Hotels, part of the multi-national Accur company. (Commercial postcard/Author's collection)

Outwards to Stoneygate

70. En route to Stoneygate, Car 115 moves along London Road past the junction with Evington Road on the right. The south coast resort of Brighton is advertised on the upper deck side panels, and a Boots store can be seen on the corner of St Albans Road; the premises now house a Domino's pizza outlet. (S. Newton)

71. Car 16 returns from Stoneygate, and has reached the Hill Top, London Road, with the tracks from Evington Road curving in from the left. 16 was previously 108, being re-numbered in September 1947, with this picture taken two years later. Following close behind is a Scammell articulated tanker owned by the Crow Carrying Company Limited fitted with single balloon tyres, other than the front steering wheels. (W.A. Camwell/National Tramway Museum)

THE STONEYGATE SERVICE

Stoneygate Tramcars from either Terminus every 4, 4¼, 5 and 6 minutes.

		Weekdays.	Saturdays.	Sundays.
First Car—Clock Tower	..	6.12 a.m.	6.12 a.m.	9.38 a.m.
,, ,, Terminus	..	6.30 a.m.	6.30 a.m.	9.57 a.m.
Last Car—Clock Tower	..	11.2¼ p.m.	11.16½ p.m.	10.47 p.m.
,, ,, Terminus	..	11.23¼ p.m.	11.37½ p.m.	11. 8 p.m.

72.   Car 20, en route to Stoneygate, seen before the large side lower window service boards were fitted, moves along London Road circa 1937, and on reaching the terminus, will return across the city to Fosse Road. The Stoneygate service operated with a frequency ranging from 4 to 6 minutes over the weekly cycle. The front advertisement announces houses for sale from £550 on the Welford Road estate. (S. Newton)

73.   At the Stoneygate terminus circa 1938, Car 42 begins the journey back to Fosse Road, whilst in the background Car 2 stands at the end of the road before reversing onto the return track. Shanklin Drive is just out of view to the immediate right, and Grenfell Road is to the left of 42; just beyond the former location stood an early six car depot, which was closed in 1922. (A.P. Newland collection)

74. This wartime picture in London Road, dating from May 1943, is of interest as it was taken by the American serviceman mentioned earlier. In the foreground, Car 16 has just arrived at the Stoneygate terminus, whilst Car 51 awaits departure to the city centre. As a wartime precaution, the headlights were masked and the word 'Leicester' painted over in order to confuse any occupying invaders. During the wartime period, trams provided 60% of the city's public transport needs. (G.F. Cunningham/National Tramway Museum)

75. This final terminus scene depicts two cars, with Car 58 in the foreground; Grenfell Road is off to the left. This picture was taken some time between May and October 1949, just before the closure of the system. With several other services already closed, the destination of 58 is not Fosse Road, but Belgrave, resulting from the remaining services being consolidated to give optimum scheduling. Note the time clock on the right. (A.D. Packer)

Outwards to Clarendon Park

Service 5 via London Road

76. Car 26 waits at the stop before leaving London Road to take the curve into Victoria Park Road, with the church of St James the Greater as the backdrop. The building is Grade II listed and was erected between 1899 and 1901, with the front structure created between 1911 and 1914. It is based on the design of the Torcello Cathedral in Venice; all the other buildings remain intact. Victoria Park is to the left, and the junction has been widened to accommodate the current traffic island. (F.N.T. Lloyd-Jones/Online Transport Archive)

CLARENDON PARK SERVICE
(*Via London Road*).

Clarendon Park Tramcars from either terminus every 4, 4½, 5 and 6 minutes (via London Road).

	Weekdays.	*Saturdays.*	*Sundays.*
First Car—Clock Tower ..	6. 8 a.m.	6. 8 a.m.	9.41 a.m.
,, ,, Welford Road ..	6.25 a.m.	6.25 a.m.	10. 0 a.m.
Last Car—Clock Tower ..	11. 0 p.m.	11.19 p.m.	10.45 p.m.
,, ,, Welford Road ..	11.18 p.m.	11.37 p.m.	11. 3 p.m.

77. Car 87 moves along Victoria Park Road towards the London Road junction circa 1933 on a cross city service to Aylestone. Victoria Park is to the right, and the car on the left is disappearing into St Mary's Road. The park was opened in 1882, but earlier had been used as a racecourse before the venue transferred to a purpose-built facility at Oadby. (Leicester Mercury/P. Hollins collection)

78. With Victoria Park in the background, Car 173 has left Victoria Park Road and entered Queens Road, which leads to Clarendon Park Road, en route to Welford Road, but displaying an incorrect Blackbird Road destination. Note the downstairs passengers are seated on lateral seating. This picture illustrates the 18in (0.45m) area beyond the outside tracks, which the department had to maintain throughout the tramway era. Wartime Nissen huts remain in the park area, which were removed in the 1950s. (F.N.T. Lloyd-Jones/Online Transport Archive)

79. Car 93 is about to enter a passing loop outside Knighton Library in Clarendon Park Road in early 1949. The passing loop allowed the location to be used as a short working facility using the overhead boom reversal wiring illustrated. (F.N.T. Lloyd Jones/Online Transport Archive)

80. At the junction of Welford Road and Clarendon Park Road on the right, a lone passenger boards Car 161. This has travelled the short distance in Welford Road along the shared track that Services 5 and 6 used from the outer terminus to where the services diverge. The shop on the corner is now a pharmacy. (F.N.T. Lloyd-Jones/Online Transport Archive)

Service 6 via Welford Road

81. Having left the Bowling Green Street city centre terminus, Car 178 has rounded the bend, and continues along Welford Road to cross the railway line that leads into the London Road station, and begins the climb up towards the Welford Road Cemetery gates in May 1945 shortly before the service closed; the cemetery is to the right of the photographer's position. Fifteen trams were fitted with special slipper brake pads to cope with the Welford Road hill on this service.
(R. Hubble/Online Transport Archive)

82. Further along Welford Road, Car 93 is seen at the stop next to the Knighton Kinema, situated on the corner with Keble Road, shortly before system closure, hence the cross-town destination of Blackbird Road. The cinema was opened in 1937 with an art deco frontage, closed in 1963, and demolished the following year; the site is now occupied by a row of uninspiring flat-roofed shops. (Lens of Sutton courtesy of A.D. Packer)

83. We have now reached the Clarendon Park terminus of the two services in Welford Road, which is situated adjacent to Gainsborough Road. Car 138 waits in the wide expanse of road, now a dual carriageway, before crossing to the inbound track where Car 161 awaits departure. The boom reversal wiring can be seen to the rear of 161. (F.E.J. Ward/Online Transport Archive)

84. In the foreground, open top Car 78, en route to Aylestone has just left Granby Street to turn into Horsefair Street, with a similar car, possibly 42, travelling in the opposite direction. On the skyline is the clock tower of the Town Hall and, on the left, the upholstery business appears to have had royal patronage indicated by the sign over the shop windows; the building is now a branch of the Natwest Bank. The curved building on the right led into the old Market Place, now the site of the Leicester Market, and on the ground floor is a shipping office. The building has now been replaced with a modern structure, which has maintained the curved profile. (Commercial postcard/Author's collection)

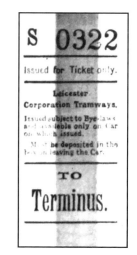

85.   Car 42 waits kerb side in the passing loop at the side of the Town Hall in Bowling Green Street on Service 5 to Aylestone in May 1938. On departure, 42 will turn right in to Belvoir Street leading in to Welford Place to join the double track in Welford Road; Bishop Street is on the left beyond the parked cars. The sign attached to the traction standard reads 'Aylestone Cars', with the stop identified by the white band.
(H.B. Priestley/
National Tramway Museum)

86. The motorman stands at the controls of balcony Car 149, previously used in the PAYE experiment, before departing to Aylestone. Above the motorman's head is the number 118, which is thought to have been the vehicle's running board number; also note the two signs attached to the traction standard, which read 'Cars Stop Here' and 'No Entrance - One Way Street'.
(A.P. Newland collection/
Leicester Transport
Heritage Trust)

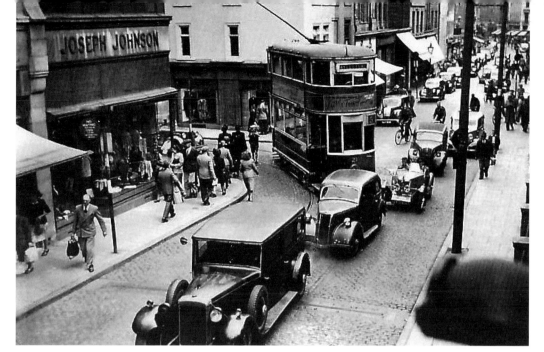

87. In this busy scene, taken in 1946, Car 21 turns out of Bowling Green Street on the tight single-track curve to enter Belvoir Street, and then onwards into Welford Place en route to Aylestone. Period cars add to the congestion, with others kerb parked further back along Belvoir Street. In the foreground is a Humber Snipe saloon followed by a Ford 8, an MG Midget open tourer, and a Ford Essex van. On the left-hand corner are the erstwhile premises of Joseph Johnson, outfitters, drapers and furnishers. (A.P. Newland collection/Leicester Transport Heritage Trust)

88. Car 54 has just left Belvoir Street and enters Welford Place on single track to move forward onto double track into Welford Road. Cars returning to the town centre could enter track in Pocklington's Walk, just out of view on the left, in order to reach Horsefair Street. In this view, the apparently unused left-hand track and overhead wiring change from double to single line suggesting an alternative return route. On the left is the statue of John Biggs (1801-1871), a radical politician who represented Leicester as an MP 1856-1862. He was also a non-conformist and philanthropist. The cyclist passes a parked 1933 Hillman Minx. (H.B. Priestley/National Tramway Museum)

89. Outside 19 Aylestone Road, Car 86, the first tram to be fully enclosed in 1924, and the only car with a normal staircase, returns to Horsefair Street, whilst passing the Freemen's Arms public house opposite Granby Halls circa 1937. In the 1890s, the pub was used as a dressing room for the Leicester Tigers rugby team. In 1994, the premises were refurbished and renamed Physio and Firkin; there were two further name changes, namely The Phizz, and the Pride of Leicester. Post 2005, the premises were demolished to provide a car park for the nearby hospital. (S. Newton)

90. At the junction of Welford and Aylestone Roads, Car 64 is on a football special duty, with a siding provided for cricket, rugby and football match day trams further out along the latter opposite Raw Dykes Road. Immediately beyond 64 is one of Leicester's 3-axle Guy CX double deck motorbuses passing a large recreation ground, part of which is now the Nelson Mandela Park. (Leicester Mercury/Leicester Transport Heritage Trust/A.P. Newland collection)

91. Car 6 has reached the siding circa 1938, and having reversed at the crossover a short distance further south, is about to turn into the facility under the watchful eye of a colleague. In addition to being adjacent to the Leicester City Football Club ground, Aylestone Road also served the Leicester Tigers Rugby Football Club and Leicestershire County Cricket Club facilities. The siding now forms the alignment of Freeman's Common Road. (A.P. Newland collection)

92. Two cars reside in the football siding circa January 1940. Car 5 in the foreground looks in a poor condition; this maybe because it was infrequently used due to the reduced headroom on the upper deck. This car was the first to be fitted with a top cover but, unlike others, did not have the lower roof reduced by 3 inches. In this view, both cars still have wartime window blackout protection, white painted areas to aid other drivers in the blackout, and 5 is fitted with a masked headlight. (N. Arnold)

93. In immaculate condition, Car 36, complete with long destination board under the lower windows, waits at the Aylestone terminus adjacent to Wigston Lane in 1937 before returning to Horsefair Street, with a second car in the background. 36 was one of 14 cars fitted with leather transverse seats in the lower saloon between 1932 and 1935. The long destination boards were introduced in the summer of 1937, and phased out at the outbreak of the Second World War; they were coloured to identify a group of services, but passengers found them confusing due to poor sequencing of the intermediate points. The property on the left is now a pizza and curry outlet. (S. Newton)

94. Car 154 has reached the end of the line in Aylestone in July 1938, and prepares to cross over to the inward bound track ready to return to the city centre. Wigston Lane leads off to the left. (W.A. Camwell/National Tramway Museum)

95. The short length of East Gates leads from High Street into the Clock Tower area, as depicted in this picture of April 1938. In the foreground, Car 84 is being held by a white-helmeted policeman to allow a horse and cart to exit from Cheapside. Corts Limited hardware store is on the right, and the White Hart Hotel can be seen in the distance beyond the Clock Tower. (Photocrom Co. Ltd)

THE AYLESTONE SERVICE

Aylestone Tramcars from either terminus every 4, 5 and 7 minutes.

		Weekdays.	Saturdays.	Sundays.
First Car—Bowling Green St.		5.52 a.m.	5.52 a.m.	9.40 a.m.
,, ,, Terminus	..	6.10 a.m.	6.10 a.m.	9.58 a.m.
Last Car—Bowling Green St.		11. 0 p.m.	11.17 p.m.	10.46 p.m.
,, ,, Terminus	..	11.18 p.m.	11.35 p.m.	11. 4 p.m.

96. Looking in the same direction as the last picture, but at the beginning of High Street, Car 60, en route to Narborough Road, leads a line of three vehicles outside Cort's hardware store circa 1937. Note the full drop upper deck windows. On the right is a shop belonging to the Fifty Shilling Tailors, who specialised in men's clothing. The business was sold to the John Collier Company in 1958, and was eventually absorbed into Burtons. (S. Newton)

→ 97. Car 110 pauses outside the High Street branch of Lloyds Bank en route to Belgrave in 1937. Wines and spirits are well represented by the shops of T. Foster and Gilby's on the right, with the former, and all the premises to the rear, using sunblinds, a feature not seen very often in today's street scene. Neither would one leave a bicycle in a city centre street as depicted on the extreme right of the picture. (S. Newton)

→ 98. Looking back towards East Gates circa 1936, Car 135 waits at the High Street loading barriers destined for Narborough Road, with a second car behind. As the inspector talks to 135's motorman, a Midland Red SOS single deck motorbus moves in the opposite direction carrying a slip board under the rear window indicating the destination as Oakham in neighbouring Rutland. (A.P. Newland collection)

99. An atmospheric early 1930s scene of the loading stands referred to in the previous picture, with an unidentified car destined for Narborough Road about to begin loading the waiting passengers. Two of the stands are for Fosse Road, reflecting their respective circular routes. Note that everyone is wearing a hat. (A.P. Newland collection/Leicester Transport Heritage Trust)

Fosse Road Circulars

The clockwise route operated as Service 4, outward via St Augustine Street and King Richards Road, and returning to the city centre via Frog Island, Northgate Street and Great Central Street. The anti-clockwise route was Service 3, and operated in the opposite direction.

100. Car 30 moves along interlaced track in King Richards Road, with the Dannett Street junction to the rear on the left circa 1938. 30 is in the new livery, and will shortly enter double track on the approach to Fosse Road. The scene is unrecognisable today, other than the property in the distance, with the road now a dual carriageway; Dannett Street is no longer connected to the main road. (S. Newton)

101. Car 156 turns out of Fosse Road Central into King Richards Road circa 1937, and will shortly enter the interlaced track referred to in the previous caption. Note the studded pedestrian crossing identified by the Belisha Beacon on the right; these crossings were introduced from 1934 by the then Minister of Transport, Leslie Hore-Belisha. The corner property was demolished to create the extra carriageway in King Richards Road. (S. Newton)

102. Car 174 appears to be leaving single track into the nearside loop in the tree-lined Fosse Road Central adjacent to Stretton Road in 1946, with Car 111 in the background. This section of road was used by cars returning to the city centre via Hinckley Road following the abandonment of the King Richards Road section on 2nd April 1939. The trees carry the black and white stripes added to assist traffic in the recent wartime blackout. (C. Carter)

103. A busy post war scene at the junction of Great Central Street, Northgate Street and Sanvey Gate, with the Great Central Hotel immediately beyond the waiting passengers on the left; Car 136 has just left Northgate Street, and begins the move along Great Central Street. Although this is the route for Services 3 and 4, 136 is displaying Service 9 (Groby Road) which used this thorough-fare for inbound journeys from early September 1937. Just leaving Sanvey Gate is a Midland Red utility Guy Arab motorbus, with a wartime Bedford tipper travelling in the opposite direction. The Austin car in the foreground makes its way towards St Nicholas Street. (F.N.T. Lloyd-Jones/Online Transport Archive)

104. Car 160 travels north along a deserted Great Central Street, with the Great Central Railway station on the left. The station opened in March 1899 and closed in May 1969; it was sited on the last north/south main line operating between London Marylebone to Nottingham and Sheffield. After the Second World War, patronage declined and, when the station closed, the platform and line areas were used by industrial units. However, the main station building seen in this picture was retained, refurbished and the inside used for several leisure activities, including a ten-pin bowling alley. (F.N.T. Lloyd-Jones/Online Transport Archive)

105. Shortly before withdrawal, and retaining the old livery, Car 110 is about to cross the bridge over the Grand Union Canal (ex Leicester Canal) on Frog Island, and enter Northgate Street inward bound from Groby Road in January 1949, with a Bedford OB coach following close behind. It was here in 1939 that Tom

Rolf, of canal fame, moored his boat to continue by tram into the city centre. 110 is displaying Service 9 and using this route for the reason explained in the caption for Picture 103. The North Bridge Tavern is to the right; the building still stands, although the premises are derelict at the time of writing. (A.P. Newland collection)

WESTERN PARK SERVICE

Western Park Tramcars from either terminus every 3, 3½, 4, 4½, 5 and 6 minutes.

		Weekdays.	Saturdays.	Sundays.
First Car—Clock Tower	..	6.15 a.m.	6.15 a.m.	9.40 a.m.
,, ,, Terminus	..	6.29 a.m.	6.29 a.m.	9.54 a.m.
Last Car—Clock Tower	..	11. 2 p.m.	11.15 p.m.	10.48 p.m.
,, ,, Terminus	..	11.16 p.m.	11.29 p.m.	11. 2 p.m.

Outwards to Western Park and Narborough Road

106. Car 118 moves along Duns Lane towards West Bridge Street on a return journey from Narborough Road whilst on Service 2 to Melton Road, and is about to cross the bridge over the Old River Soar. The factory in the background was owned by Frisby-Jarvis, who were hosiery manufacturers, with Case's Cash Store on the left. The advertising hoardings carry advertisements for the Westleigh and Savoy cinemas, plus the Territorial Army. (A.P. Newland collection)

107. Car 26 passes the Hinckley Road/Narborough Road junction en route to Western Park circa 1946, with a second car travelling in the opposite direction. 26 was one of 23 cars to receive new frames and extended platforms to speed up loading and unloading, and one of 14 to be fitted with transverse leather seats in the lower saloon. A lorry belonging to W. Canning Limited, who produced electroplating and polishing equipment, leaves Narborough Road loaded with caskets in protective frames. Note the police box to the right of the seated gentlemen, with what appears to be a policeman's bicycle stood outside. (A.P. Newland collection/Leicester Transport Heritage Trust)

108. Car 32 has reached the bottom of Hinckley Road, and is about to pass Narborough Road on the right before joining Braunstone Gate. At the time the photograph was taken the Shipstone's Arms public house was on the corner of Great Holme Street, which no longer exists, and had a conveniently placed car stop outside. The landlord at the time was a Mr Arthur E. Johnson. Shipstone's Brewery closed in 1991, although the brand continued for a few years afterwards. (F.N.T. Lloyd-Jones/Online Transport Archive)

109. Car 139 travels along Hinckley Road near the junction with Clarefield Road whilst returning from Western Park en route to Belgrave in January 1948 as the motorman looks towards the photographer. As the date of the eventual closure of the system drew nearer, and services were gradually being converted to motorbus, the remaining tram services were frequently consolidated to provide operational efficiency. On the left, a Leicester all Leyland PD1 (247) double deck motorbus travels in the opposite direction. (A.P. Newland collection)

110. On a wet day, Car 101 has reached the Western Park terminus adjacent to Western Park Road in 1938, and will soon reverse across to the inward track with the boom swinging round via the triangular overhead wiring in front of the tree; following close behind is Car 116. The entrance to the park, which was purchased by the Corporation in 1897 for £30,000, is to the immediate left of the photographer's position. One of the five art deco passenger shelters referred to earlier was located at this terminus. (W.A. Camwell/National Tramway Museum)

111. Car 108 has left the Hinckley Road/Narborough Road junction, and approaching the Narborough Road terminus has stopped in the latter close to Harlaxton Street in March 1935. Having dismounted from the motorman's end of the car, the two ladies are faced with crossing the road to the far pavement avoiding the Vauxhall car and other overtaking traffic.
(Leicester Mercury/ P. Hollins collection)

NARBOROUGH ROAD SERVICE

Narborough Road Tramcars from either Terminus every 3, 3½, 4, 4½, 5 and 6 minutes.

		Weekdays.	Saturdays.	Sundays.
First Car—Clock Tower	..	6.10 a.m.	6.10 a.m.	9.37¼ a.m.
,, ,, Terminus	..	6.24 a.m.	6.24 a.m.	9.51¼ a.m.
Last Car—Clock Tower	..	11.4½ p.m.	11.17 p.m.	10.46 p.m.
,, ,, Terminus	..	11.18½ p.m.	11.31 p.m.	11. 0 p.m.

112. At the Narborough Road terminus in April 1939, Car 145 waits to return to Melton Road, with the destination displays already altered for this destination. Below the central window is the long slip board indicating the service route, which were dispensed with at the outbreak of the Second World War. On the right, note one of the five art deco passenger shelters.
(M.J. O'Connor/National Tramway Museum)

DECORATED CARS

113. Over the years, Leicester decorated cars to commemorate, or promote, a series of events. In this picture, the theme was the benefits of keeping fit, and Car 48, seen at the Aylestone terminus in November 1938, is adorned with a variety of advertisements. One makes the citizens aware of a forthcoming event at the De Montfort Hall, when the then Health Minister, Sir Kingsley Wood, will speak on the 'National Health Campaign'. Other attractions are the use of an organ, plus a Health and Beauty demonstration. From a health point of view, it was unfortunate that the photograph was taken with the Gold Flake cigarette advertisement on the left.
(A.P. Newland collection/
Leicester Transport Heritage Trust)

Xh4347

Belgrave		Humber-stone
Melton Rd.		Melbourne Hall
St. Barnabas' Church		Fosse Rd.
Evington Road		Mid. Rly. Station
Stoneygate		Gt North's Rly. Stat'n
Narboro' Road		Slater Street
Western Park		Coblen St.
Groby Rd.		Narboro' Rd Juncty
Aylestone		Welford Rd Junction
Clarendon Park		Horsefair Street
Depot		Tower

Leicester Corporation Tramways.
TRANSFER OR RETURN TICKET.
EXCHANGE FOR

Issued subject to Bye-laws.

A 0865
Leicester
Corporation Tramways.

EXCESS FARE,

·1d.

P-A Y E Ticket.

I 2501

RETURN TICKET.

FARE, 1D.

Corporation Tramways.

This Ticket is available for
return . . . . m.
(Saturday . . . Day), on
day of issue.

Not transferable.

Issued subject to Bye-laws.

NARBO . . . MINUS

CLO . . . ER

and RETURN.

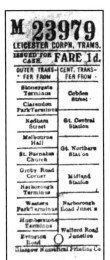

M 23979

LEICESTER CORPN. TRAMS.

ISSUED FOR CASH — FARE 1d.

OUTER TRANS-FER FROM	CENT. TRANS-FER FROM
Stoneygate Terminus	Cobden Street
Clarendon Park Terminus	
Northam Street	Gt. Central Station
Melbourne Hall	
St. Barnabas Church	Gt. Northern Station
Groby Road Corner	Midland Station
Narborough Terminus	
Western Park Terminus	Narborough Road Junct'n
Humberstone Terminus	Welford Road Junction
Evington Road	

Glasgow Numerical Printing Co

114. Car 58 was specially decorated to be used at the closure of Leicester's tram system. During just over 45 years of the system's existence, the astounding mileage and passenger figures achieved by the trams can be seen. The system closed on 9th November 1949 and, after a return trip from Humberstone, 58 left the Humberstone Gate Central depot with the official party to travel for the final time to Abbey Park Road depot. This last journey was driven by ex-motorman, Jack White, who drove Leicester's first electric tram in 1904.

(R.E. Tustin/via R.P. Hendry Archive/Elrokits)

DEPOTS

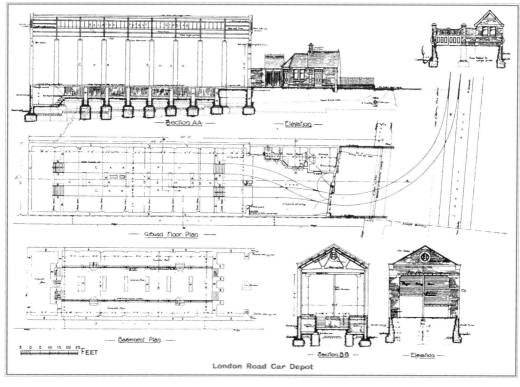

London Road Car Depot

← 115. This picture inside the Abbey Park Road depot has several points of interest. Cars 127 and 74 are parked over the inspection pits, with two further cars on the extreme left; 127 is in the new livery introduced in 1937, and 74 in the old. Also in the picture are two of the three water cars used to carry out a variety of functions, including track and gutter swilling, rail grinding, snow clearing and depot shunting. After a series of renumberings, they finally finished up with fleet numbers 179-181, with the latter fitted with a tower used for overhead wire maintenance over the reserved track in Blackbird Road. (H.B. Priestley/National Tramway Museum)

116. The 'Hole in the Wall'. This is the entrance to the Humberstone Gate Central Depot in September 1949, with the Transport Department's office on the left, and the public bar of the Bell Hotel on the right. Car 16 enters the single track leading to five tracks that could accommodate cars used mainly for peak hour duties. Originally the site was a permanent way store, a traffic control office and motor garage, but converted to accommodate 13 cars when the small satellite depots at Stoneygate and Narborough Road were closed in 1922. (F.N.T. Lloyd-Jones/ Online Transport Archive)

← *Plan of Stoneygate Sub Depot.*

EMPLOYEES

Rather than show the normal group images of operational staff, the next two pictures illustrate some of the many staff who worked behind the scenes to maintain the fleet to a high standard.

117. Here we see the Body Shop circa 1916, with two tradesmen working on the front of a damaged car. Note the semi-circular component on the left, which presumably will be fitted to form the front bumper. (Leicester Transport Heritage Trust)

118. Three fitters remove an electric motor from a truck with the aid of an overhead hoist in February 1943. Note the gear wheel on the output shaft of the motor, the large gears on the front axle and Car 78 in the background. (Leicester Transport Heritage Trust)

THE AFTERLIFE

119. Preserved Car 76, held at the Tramway Village, Crich, Derbyshire, stands with two other vehicles that had a Leicester connection. Tower wagon BC 1078 is a solid-tyred Leyland which, together with two other similar vehicles, maintained the overhead infrastructure and its subsequent removal after the system closed. On the right is one of the 25 AEC Renown 3-axle motorbuses (329) that the pre-war General Manager specified for the initial phase of the tram conversion programme. The remains of Car 31 are currently stored pending a long-term restoration programme by the 'Tram 31 Group'. The 1904 depot at Stoneygate still exists, and is managed by the Leicester Transport Heritage Trust. It is regularly open to the public to display Leicester tram related items, and has been awarded a Transport Trust 'Red Wheel' acknowledging it as a rare example of a 'District Car Shed'. (A.P. Newland/Leicester Transport Heritage Trust)

National Tramway Museum,
Crich, Matlock,
Derbyshire, DE4 5DP
https://www.tramway.co.uk/
Telephone: 01773 854 321

Leicester Heritage
Transport Trust,
453 London Road,
Leicester, LE2 3RG
https://ltht.org.uk/

WHAT MIGHT HAVE BEEN

120. In 1930, Leicester obtained powers to operate trolleybuses along any road where they operated trams, and so began a long running debate as to whether the trams should be replaced by this form of traction, or by motorbuses. The Transport Department favoured the latter, but the Electricity Committee wanted to convert to trolleybuses, no doubt worried by the potential loss of load from the municipal power station. Strong representations were made by both sides, and in October 1934 the then General Manager, Hubert Pool, submitted a report recommending the use of motorbuses, notwithstanding a visit to Huddersfield made by Leicester officials to see the town's trolleybuses in operation.

The debate continued and, in October 1937, a new General Manager, Ben England, submitted a report again recommending motorbuses using high seating capacity vehicles; he noted that the Electricity Department had been grossly overcharging for tram traction power, which triggered a supplementary report. Finally, in February 1938, the City Council took the decision to convert the tram system to motorbus operation.

In the picture above, the rear of a London Transport trolleybus has been superimposed on a view of the Clock Tower to illustrate this type of vehicle in the city. Stoneygate has been added to the destination display, together with a Leicester registration number. However, a London Transport trolleybus logo can be seen at the bottom of the rear panel. Incorrectly spaced trolleybus overhead wiring has also been added; if implemented, the overhead infrastructure around the Clock Tower would have been extremely complex. (A.P. Newland collection/Leicester Transport Heritage Trust)

FLEET LIST

Fleet No.	Type	Year(s)	Builder	Seats	4 Wheel Truck
2 1/3-99	Open Top	1903	Brush	22/34	Brush 21E
	Open Top	1903-04	ER&TCW	22/34	Brill 21E
	• Fitted with top covers by 1929. • Apart from 12, 24, 29 & 44 all fully enclosed by 1934. • 8, 6, & 20 re-numbered 162, 108 & 8 in 1947. • 86 rebuilt fully enclosed 1923. Seating became 22/36. • 2 not used; became 191 to London Metropolitan.				
101-121	Covered Balcony	1905	UEC	22/34	Brill 21E
	• Fully enclosed by 1934.				
122-141	Open Top	1905	UEC	22/34	Brill 21E
	• Fitted with top covers 1910-11. • Apart from 122 & 128 all fully enclosed by 1934. • 137 re-numbered 100 & 141 became 137 in 1911.				
141-150	Covered Balcony	1913	UEC	22/38	Brill 21E
	• P.A.Y.E. Subsequently fully enclosed.				
151-160	Covered Balcony	1914	Brush	22/38	Brill 21E
	• Subsequently fully enclosed.				
161-166	Covered Balcony	1920	LCT	22/34	Preston Std 21E
	• 162 renumbered 20 in 1947. • 177 re-numbered 115 in 1948. • Subsequently fully enclosed.				
167-178	Covered Balcony	1920	EE	22/34	Preston Std 21E
	• Subsequently fully enclosed.				
179	Water Car	1904	ER&TCW	-	Brill 21E
	• Originally 100. • Re-numbered 141 in 1912 and 179 in 1920.				
180	Water Car	1905	UEC	-	Brill 21E
	• Originally 142. • Re-numbered 152 in 1912 and 180 in 1920.				
181	Water Car	1909	UEC	-	Brill 21E
	• Originally 143. • Re-numbered 153 in 1912 and 181 in 1920. • Fitted with tower platform for Blackbird Rd overhead.				

All cars were double deck with reversed staircase and two axle trucks; subsequently top covers were fitted to open top vehicles. This was followed by various experiments to give weather protection to open balcony areas and motormen, culminating in a conversion programme to provide all cars with a fully enclosed specification.

Experiments were conducted with a PAYE scheme, and the use of bow and pantograph current collection; none were pursued.

Middleton Press

126a Camelsdale Road, Haslemere, Surr
GU27 3RJ   Tel:01730 813169
■ MAIL ORDER ■
email:info@middletonpress.co.uk

ISBN PREFIXES - A-978 0 906520 B- 978 1 873793 C- 978 1 901706 D-978 1 904474 E - 978 1 906008 F - 978 1 908174 G - 978 1 91035

PLEASE VISIT OUR WEBSITE - www.middletonpress.co.uk - OR REQUEST A BROCHUF
TO CHECK AVAILABILITY OF THESE AND OTHER RAILWAY ALBUMS AND NEW TITLES

TRAMWAY CLASSICS Editor Robert J Harley

Title		Code
Aldgate & Stepney Tramways to Hackney and West India Docks		B 70 1
Barnet & Finchley Tramways to Golders Green and Highgate		B 93 0
Bath Tramways Peter Davey and Paul Welland	(OOS)	B 86 2
Blackpool Tramways 1933-66 75 years of Streamliners Stephen Lockwood	(OOS)	E 34 5
Bournemouth & Poole Tramways Roy C Anderson		B 47 3
Brightons Tramways The Corporation's routes plus lines to Shoreham and Rottingdean	(OOS)	B 02 2
Bristol's Tramways A massive system radiating to ten destinations Peter Davey	(OOS)	B 57 2
Burton & Ashby Tramways An often rural light railway Peter M White		C 51 2
Camberwell & West Norwood Trys including Herne Hill and Peckham Rye		B 22 0
Chester Tramways Barry M Marsden		E 04 8
Chesterfield Tramways a typical provincial system Barry Marsden		D 37 1
Clapham & Streatham Tramways inc Tooting & Earlsfield J.Gent & J.Meredith	(OOS)	B 97 8
Colchester Tramways the untold story	(OOS)	G 31 9
Croydons Tramways J.Gent & J.Meredith including Crystal Palace, Mitcham and Sutton		B 42 8
Derby Tramways a comprehensive city system Colin Barker		D 17 3
Dover's Tramways to River and Maxton		B 24 4
East Ham & West Ham Trys from Stratford and Ilford down to the docks		B 52 7
Edgware & Willesden Tramways including Sudbury, Paddington & Acton		C 18 5
Eltham & Woolwich Tramways	(OOS)	B 74 9
Embankment & Waterloo Trys including the fondly remembered Kingsway Subway		B 41 1
Enfield and Wood Green Tramways Dave Jones	(OOS)	C 03 1
Exeter & Taunton Tramways Two charming small systems J B Perkin		B 32 9
Fulwell - Home for Trams, Trolleys and Buses Professor Bryan Woodriff		D 11 1
Gosport & Horndean Tramways Martin Petch		B 92 3
Great Yarmouth Tramways A seaside pleasure trip Dave Mackley		D 13 5
Hammersmith & Hounslow Trys branches to Hanwell, Acton & Shepherds Bush		C 33 8
Hampstead & Highgate Trys from Tottenham Court Road and King's Cross Dave Jones		B 53 4
Hastings Tramways A sea front and rural ride		B 18 3
Holborn & Finsbury Trys Angel-Balls Pond Road - Moorgate - Bloomsbury		B 79 4
Huddersfield Tramways the original municipal system Stephen Lockwood		D 95 1
Hull Tramways Level crossings and bridges abound Paul Morfitt & Malcolm Wells		D 60 9
Ilford & Barking Tramways to Barkingside, Chadwell Heath and Beckton		B 61 9
Ilkeston & Glossop Tramways Barry M Marsden		D 40 1
Ipswich Tramways Colin Barker		E 55 0
Keighley Tramways & Trolleybuses Barry M Marsden		D 83 8
Kingston & Wimbledon Trys incl Hampton Court, Tooting & four routes from Kingston		B 56 5
Leicester Tramways Colin Barker		G 83 8
Liverpool Tramways - 1 Eastern Routes	(OOS)	C 04 8
Liverpool Tramways - 2 Southern Routes	(OOS)	C 23 9
Liverpool Tramways - 3 Northern Routes A triliogy by Brian Martin		C 46 8
Llandudno & Colwyn Bay Tramways Stephen Lockwood		E 17 8
Lowestoft Tramways a seaside system David Mackley		E 74 1
Maidstone & Chatham Trys from Barming to Loose and from Strood to Rainham		B 40 4
Margate & Ramsgate Tramways including Broadstairs		C 52 9
North Kent Tramways including Bexley, Erith, Dartford, Gravesend and Sheerness		B 44 2
Norwich Tramways A popular system comprising ten main routes David Mackley		C 40 6
Nottingham's First Generation Tramways Colin Barker		G 73 9
Nottinghamshire & Derbyshire Try including the Matlock Cable Tramway Barry M Marsden		D 53 1
Plymouth and Torquay Trys including Babbacombe Cliff Lift Roy Anderson		E 97 0

Title		Code
Portsmouth Tramways including Southsea Martin Petch		B ?
Reading Tramways Three routes - a comprehensive coverage Edgar Jordon		B ?
Scarborough Tramway including the Scarborough Cliff Lifts Barry M Marsden		E ?
Seaton & Eastbourne Tramways Attractive miniature lines		B 7
Shepherds Bush & Uxbridge Tramways inc Ealing John C Gillham	(OOS)	C 2
Southend-on-Sea Tramways including the Pier Electric Railway		B ?
South London Tramways 1903-33 Wandsworth - Dartford		D ?
South London Tramways 1933-52 The Thames to Croydon		D ?
Southampton Tramways Martin Petch	(OOS)	B 3
Southwark & Deptford Tramways including the Old Kent Road		B 3
Stamford Hill Tramways including Stoke Newington and Liverpool Street		B 8
Triumphant Tramways of England Stephen Lockwood FULL COLOUR	(OOS)	E 6
Twickenham & Kingston Trys extending to Richmond Bridge and Wimbledon		C 3
Victoria & Lambeth Tramways to Nine Elms, Brixton and Kennington		B 4
Waltham Cross & Edmonton Trys to Finsbury Park, Wood Green and Enfield		C 0
Walthamstow & Leyton Trys including Clapton, Chingford Hill and Woodford		B 6
Wandsworth & Battersea Trys from Hammersmith, Putney and Chelsea		B 6
York Tramways & Trolleybuses Barry M Marsden		D ?

TROLLEYBUSES (all limp covers)

Title		Code
Birmingham Trolleybuses ... David Harvey		E ?
Bournemouth Trolleybuses ... Malcolm N Pearce	(OOS)	C ?
Bradford Trolleybuses ... Stephen Lockwood		D ?
Brighton Trolleybuses ... Andrew Henbest		D ?
Cardiff Trolleybuses ... Stephen Lockwood		D ?
Chesterfield Trolleybuses ... Barry M Marsden		D ?
Croydon Trolleybuses ... Terry Russell		B 7
Darlington Trolleybuses ... Stephen Lockwood		D ?
Derby Trolleybuses ... Colin Barker	(OOS)	C 7
Doncaster Trolleybuses ... Colin Barker		E 9
Glasgow Trolleybuses ... Colin Barker		F 9
Grimsby & Cleethorpes Trolleybuses ... Colin Barker		D ?
Hastings Trolleybuses ... Lyndon W Rowe	(OOS)	B 8
Huddersfield Trolleybuses ... Stephen Lockwood		C 9
Hull Trolleybuses ... Paul Morfitt and Malcolm Wells		D ?
Ipswich Trolleybuses ... Colin Barker		D ?
Maidstone Trolleybuses ... Robert J Harley		C 0
Manchester & Ashton Trolleybuses ... Stephen Lockwood		E 7
Mexborough & Swinton Trolleybuses ... Colin Barker		E 3
Newcastle Trolleybuses ... Stephen Lockwood	(OOS)	D ?
Nottingham Trolleybuses ... Colin Barker	(OOS)	F 7
Nottinghamshire & Derbyshire Trolleybuses ... Barry M Marsden		D ?
Portsmouth Trolleybuses ... Barry Cox	(OOS)	C 7
Reading Trolleybuses ... David Hall	(OOS)	C 0
Rotherham Trolleybuses ... Colin Barker		F 4
Southend Trolleybuses ... Colin Barker		F 2
South Lancashire Trolleybuses ... Stephen Lockwood	(OOS)	F 3
South Shields Trolleybuses ... Stephen Lockwood		E 1
St. Helens Trolleybuses ... Stephen Lockwood		F 4
Tees-side Trolleybuses ... Stephen Lockwood		D 5
Walsall Trolleybuses ... Stephen Lockwood	(OOS)	F 6
Wolverhampton Trolleybuses 1961-67 ... Graham Sidwell		D 8
Woolwich and Dartford Trolleybuses ... Robert J Harley		B 6